IMMIGRATION

BLESSING OR BURDEN?

Robert Morrow

Lerner Publications Company
Minneapolis

Library of Congress Cataloging-in-Publication Data

Morrow, Robert.
    Immigration : burden or blessing? / Robert Morrow.
      p. cm.
    Includes bibliographical references and index.
    Summary: Discusses the pros and cons of immigration.
    ISBN 0-8225-2613-1 (alk. paper)
    1. United States—Emigration and immigration—Juvenile literature.
    2. Immigrants—United States—Juvenile literature. [1. United
    States—Emigration and immigration.] I. Title.
    JV6450.M67 1997   97-3708
    304.8'0973—dc21

Manufactured in the United States of America
1 2 3 4 5 6 – JR – 02 01 00 99 98 97

CONTENTS

FOREWORD

If a nation expects to be ignorant and free, . . . it expects what never was and never will be.

Thomas Jefferson

Are you ready to participate in forming the policies of our government? Many issues are very confusing, and it can be difficult to know what to think about them or how to make a decision about them. Sometimes you must gather information about a subject before you can be informed enough to make a decision. Bernard Baruch, a prosperous American financier and an advisor to every president from Woodrow Wilson to Dwight D. Eisenhower, said, "If you can get all the facts, your judgment can be right; if you don't get all the facts, it can't be right."

But gathering information is only one part of the decision-making process. The way you interpret information is influenced by the values you have been taught since infancy—ideas about right and wrong, good and bad. Many of your values are shaped, or at least influenced, by how and where you grow up, by your race, sex, and religion, by how much money your family has. What your parents believe, what they read, and what you read and believe influence your decisions. The values of friends and teachers also affect what you think.

It's always good to listen to the opinions of people around you, but you will often confront contradictory points of view and points of view that are based not on fact, but on myth. John F. Kennedy, the 35th president of the United States, said, "The great enemy of the truth is very often not the lie—deliberate, contrived, and dishonest—but the myth—persistent, persuasive, and unrealistic." Eventually you will have to separate fact from myth and make up your own mind, make your own decisions. Because you are responsible for your decisions, it's im-

4

portant to get as much information as you can. Then your decisions will be the right ones for you.

Making a fair and informed decision can be an exciting process, a chance to examine new ideas and different points of view. You live in a world that changes quickly and sometimes dramatically—a world that offers the opportunity to explore the ever-changing ground between yourself and others. Instead of forming a single, easy, or popular point of view, you might develop a rich and complex vision that offers new alternatives. Explore the many dimensions of an idea. Find kinship among an extensive range of opinions. Only after you've done this should you try to form your own opinions.

After you have formed an opinion about a particular subject, you may believe it is the only right decision. But some people will disagree with you and challenge your beliefs. They are not trying to antagonize you or put you down. They probably believe that they're right as sincerely as you believe you are. Thomas Macaulay, an English historian and author, wrote, "Men are never so likely to settle a question rightly as when they discuss it freely." In a democracy, the free exchange of ideas is not only encouraged, it's vital. Examining and discussing public issues and understanding opposing ideas are desirable and necessary elements of a free nation's ability to govern itself.

The Pro/Con series is designed to explore and examine different points of view on contemporary issues and to help you develop an understanding and appreciation of them. Most importantly, it will help you form your own opinions and make your own honest, informed decision.

Mary Winget
Series Editor

THE IMMIGRATION DILEMMA

What makes the United States of America different from any other country on earth? Is it baseball, football, MTV, computer games, or in-line skating? All of these things are uniquely American, but the one thing that makes the United States really different from any other country is that all the people who live here are immigrants or descendants of immigrants. Immigrants are people who move from their own lands to make a home in a new country. Even those Native Americans who lived here long before the first Europeans arrived are descended from nomads who made their way across the Bering Strait thousands of years ago.

The early history of the United States is a story of growth and expansion. In 1620, the *Mayflower*—a ship carrying English pilgrims—arrived at Plymouth Rock, in what is now Massachusetts. Joined by other immigrants from England and Europe, these early settlers built 13 colonies, fought the Revolutionary War with England, declared their independence in 1776, and founded the United States of America.

This Currier & Ives lithograph depicts the pilgrims arriving at Plymouth, Massachusetts, on December 22, 1620.

Soon, more people came to make a home here. Over the years they built cities, factories, and railroads until the United States stretched from the Atlantic Ocean to the Pacific Ocean and became the wealthiest, most powerful nation on earth. The United States became known as a "melting pot" because of the vast array of races, cultures, and ethnic groups that helped build it.

On the surface, America's history of immigration might appear quite peaceful and orderly. In reality, however, the story of immigration reflects a rough and rocky history. New immigrants have not always been welcomed by those already here. In fact, Benjamin Franklin, a founding father and one of our most historically revered patriots, once engaged in "immigrant bashing" himself. Franklin, a not-too-distant descendant of English immigrants, was angry about the intrusion of German settlers in Pennsylvania. "Why should the Palatine *Boors*," Franklin asked, referring to the Rhenish Palatinate—a German region that was the birthplace of many new Pennsylvania settlers—"be suffered to swarm into our Settlements, and by herding together, establish their Language and Manners to the Exclusion of ours? Why should *Pennsylvania,* founded by the *English,* become a Colony of *Aliens?*"[1]

Sometimes the melting pot boils over because of controversy about immigration. Many Americans argue that new immigrants cling to their own languages, customs, and cultures, refusing to become "Americanized." Cultural diversity—also called multiculturalism—sometimes seems to threaten national cohesiveness, the ability to live and act as a single nation. But the issue of "Americanization" is only one of many issues that have fueled the hotly debated immigration dilemma. Other pressing issues revolve around economic, moral, and social considerations, and especially around the problem of illegal immigration.

Illegal immigrants are people who enter the United States without permission from the Immigration and Naturalization Service (INS), the federal agency charged with controlling the number of immigrants who enter the country. About 2 million illegal immigrants from Mexico and Latin America have poured into the state of California within the last 10 years.

In a country with a population approaching 300 million people, the presence of additional immigrants, both legal and illegal, has angered many Americans already faced with a shortage of good jobs, an unstable

A Polish language bookstore in Brooklyn, New York. Some Americans think immigrants should not cling to their native language.

economy, and a high crime rate. Many people believe that our population has grown so much that we don't need—nor can we accommodate—any more people from foreign countries. These opponents of immigration say that immigrants, especially illegal immigrants from Mexico and the Caribbean, have swelled the ranks of welfare recipients, further draining our already strained economy. Immigrants, they argue, rob deserving Americans of jobs, and crime flourishes where there is a large influx of immigrants, especially illegal aliens.

Some politicians, such as Governor Pete Wilson of California, have called for drastically reduced numbers of legal immigrants and harsh measures to curtail illegal immigration. The measures proposed by Wilson

This demonstration opposes measures that would reduce the number of legal immigrants allowed in the United States.

and other immigration opponents would deny basic medical care and public schooling to illegal immigrants and would require every American citizen to carry a national identity card. Some opponents even argue that the Fourteenth Amendment, which guarantees citizenship to anyone born in the United States, should be repealed.

Other people support immigration, however. They see a country whose very foundation is built on its immigrant heritage. In a special issue devoted to "America's Immigration Challenge," the editors of *Time* magazine wrote, "The present popular discontent may produce some needed changes in immigration laws and practices. But there is no turning back: diversity breeds diversity. It is the fuel that runs. . . America, and, in a world being transformed daily by technologies that render distances meaningless, it puts America at the forefront of a new international order."[2]

Two poems, one famous, the other virtually unknown, put the immigration dilemma in perspective. Emma Lazarus wrote a poem that is inscribed on a plaque at the base of the Statue of Liberty in New York Harbor. It reads, in part:

> . . . Here at our sea-washed, sunset gates shall stand
> A mighty woman with a torch, whose flame
> Is the imprisoned lightning, and her name
> Mother of Exiles. From her beacon-hand
> Glows world-wide welcome; her mild eyes command
> The air-bridged harbor that twin cities frame.
> "Keep ancient lands, your storied pomp!" cries she
> With silent lips. "Give me your tired, your poor,
> Your huddled masses yearning to breathe free,
> The wretched refuse of your teeming shore.
> Send these, the homeless, tempest-tost to me—
> I lift my lamp beside the golden door!"[3]

The second poem, by an anonymous author, is undated, but it conveys a familiar attitude about immigrants. It reads:

> We thank Thee, Lord, that by Thy grace
> Thou brought us to this lovely place.
> And now dear Lord we humbly pray
> Thou wilt all others keep away.

The immigration debate does not represent a single problem with a single solution. Rather, it is a complex issue with many, sometimes overlapping components. Among these components are social, economic, moral, and cultural considerations. To fully understand the

The Statue of Liberty, on Liberty Island in New York Harbor, is a symbol of the United States and a beacon of freedom for many immigrants.

issue requires a review of the history of immigration and immigration policy, a close look at what immigrants may or may not contribute to the well-being of America, a sampling of public opinion, and a study of the illegal immigration dilemma.

Many Cubans risk their lives to gain entry into the United States. These Cuban refugees wave to a U.S. Coast Guard helicopter as they float on a raft in the Florida Straits.

WHO ARE THEY AND WHERE DO THEY COME FROM?

Why have people immigrated to the United States? If you could ask that question of a thousand immigrants, each would probably give one of three basic reasons:

- They wanted to immigrate because the United States offered opportunity and a chance for growth and economic gain.
- They were driven by war, famine, economic hardship, or religious or political persecution to leave their homelands.
- They were forced to come here.

The last reason reflects a particularly bleak chapter in U.S. history that occurred between the arrival of the first English settlers in the early 1600s and the Civil War (1860–1865). During that period, slave traders transported more than a half-million native Africans to the New World and sold them into bondage. Although legislation in 1808 banned further importation of

A slave trader guided a group of captured people to a slave station in central Africa. From there, the people were sent to the United States and sold as slaves.

slaves to the United States, it did not help those already in bondage. Furthermore, a brisk market for slaves smuggled into the country continued until the outbreak of the Civil War in 1860. It was not until 1865 that slavery was finally abolished. More than 30 million Americans can trace their heritage to Africa.[1]

But what of the very first immigrants? Why did they come, thousands of years ago, to this vast, unpopulated continent?

THE FIRST ARRIVALS

Anthropologists say that the first immigrants, the ancestors of American Indians, arrived on the North American continent during the ice age, sometime between 30,000 B.C. and 12,000 B.C. They crossed the Bering Strait on a land bridge that then connected

Alaska to Siberia. They were nomads, or wanderers, who came here seeking animals for food and fur.[2] By the time water covered the land bridge, the first wave of immigrants had become established. Eventually the newcomers built a trade center of 40,000 people near what is now St. Louis, Missouri—almost 300 years before Columbus "discovered" the New World.[3]

By 1492, when Christopher Columbus made his historic voyage, there were about 20 million people spread across North and South America. They practiced various religions and cultures and spoke about 900 different languages. About 1 million Indians, representing 2,000 tribes, occupied the land that eventually became the United States.[4]

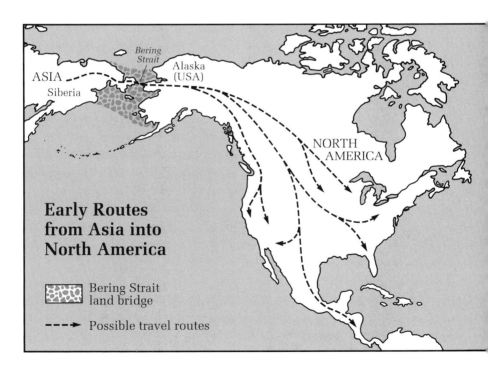

Early Routes from Asia into North America

ASIA
Siberia
Bering Strait
Alaska (USA)
NORTH AMERICA

Bering Strait land bridge

Possible travel routes

Following Columbus, European explorers ventured to the New World to seek fortune and establish settlements that later became great cities.

THE AGE OF EXPLORATION AND EXPANSION

Although many Americans trace their cultural heritage to the English settlements of the 1600s, it is important to note that a century before the English arrived in Jamestown, Virginia, in 1607, the Spanish had already established numerous settlements and cities in Central America and South America.

In 1513, the Spanish built a colony near Saint Augustine, Florida. In search of gold, a Spanish expedition traveled through what is now Georgia, South Carolina, North Carolina, Tennessee, Alabama, Arkansas, and Louisiana. The Spanish then conquered much of Mexico and the American Southwest. Spanish settlers also established the cities of San Diego (1542),

Spanish explorers searched for gold in the New World. They conquered much of Mexico and what is now the southwestern United States.

French fur traders established many trading centers, such as this one at Fort Pitt in Canada.

San Francisco (1776), and Los Angeles (1781) in California. The city of Santa Fe, New Mexico, was founded in 1609 or 1610 as the capital of the Spanish colony of New Mexico.

French fur traders also explored North America. From the shore of the Atlantic Ocean, they followed a route up the St. Lawrence River and founded the city of Quebec in 1608. The French continued their exploration in 1682, traveling down the Mississippi River from the Great Lakes. They established several French-Indian trading centers along the river, including one large center that became St. Louis, Missouri. In 1718, the French founded the city of New Orleans, where the Mississippi meets the Gulf of Mexico.

In 1803, an important event, the Louisiana Purchase, took place. In this transaction, the United States bought more than 825,000 square miles of land from France for about $15 million. The area stretched from the Mississippi River to the Rocky Mountains and from the Gulf of Mexico to the Canadian border. All or part of 15 states were later formed from territory included in the Louisiana Purchase.

EARLY AMERICA: 1608–1820

While the Spanish and French were exploring the interior and western portions of North America, the English were building the 13 original colonies along the coast of the Atlantic Ocean. Among the first arrivals during the 1600s were black slaves and indentured servants, both black and white. Indentured servants signed a contract to work without wages for a master for a specified period of time. It usually took them four to seven years to pay the cost of their transportation to the New World.

In 1680, fewer than 200,000 people were living in colonial America.[5] Between 1700 and the beginning of the Revolutionary War, fewer immigrants came from England, but the number from Germany, Ireland, and Scotland increased sharply. By 1776, when the colonies declared their independence from England, an estimated 2.5 million people lived in the New World, including a half-million slaves. The newcomers spread throughout the colonies—the Welsh and Germans in Pennsylvania and the Carolinas, the Swedes and Finns in Delaware, Sephardic Jews in Rhode Island, the Dutch in New York, and the French in South Carolina and most major New England towns.[6]

New immigrants, however, were not always wel-

Michel-Guillaume-Jean de Crèvecoeur was an eighteenth-century French immigrant.

comed by those already here. For example, Roman Catholics were discouraged from settling in some largely Protestant areas of New England, even though they were not actually prohibited from doing so.[7] The more established residents complained about the intrusion of new, foreign-speaking, foreign-acting settlers.

Still, tolerance prevailed, and in 1782, French immigrant Michel-Guillaume-Jean de Crèvecoeur wrote of the colonists:

> What then is the American, this new man? He is either an [sic] European, or the descendant of a European, hence that strange mixture of blood, which you will find in no other country. I could point out to you a family whose grandfather was an Englishman, whose wife was Dutch, whose son married a French woman, and whose present four sons now have four wives of different nations. . . . Here individuals of all nations are melted into a new race of men, whose labours and posterity will one day cause great changes in the world.[8]

IMMIGRATION SLOWS TO A TRICKLE: 1783–1815

Between 1783 and 1815, immigration to America almost came to a halt. Only 250,000 people arrived during that 22-year period.[9] The decline was due in part to the fact that England, which had lost the American Revolutionary War, now discouraged emigration (leaving one country for another). Wars in Europe and America also slowed immigration and made passage by ship across the Atlantic Ocean hazardous. During the War of 1812, immigration came to a virtual stop.[10]

A NEW WAVE OF IMMIGRANTS: 1820–1870

A new wave of immigrants, most from Ireland and Germany, arrived between 1820 and 1890. Westward expansion in America, famine and poverty in Ireland, and political upheaval in Germany brought roughly 5 million European immigrants to the United States during the 1800s—more people than the entire immigrant population in 1790, when the first census had been taken.[11]

The first great wave of immigrants, often called "old immigrants" by historians, arrived during a time when America's doors were open to anyone who could buy a boat ticket or walk across the country's borders. As George Washington, the first president of the United States, had proclaimed, "The bosom of America is open . . . to the oppressed and persecuted of all Nations and Religions."[12]

Washington's words were eloquent, but in reality, many of the old immigrants had not been welcomed. In addition to the immigrants from northern and western Europe, about 300,000 Chinese and 90,000 Japanese

Nineteenth-century German and Irish immigrants mingle on the Battery, a section of New York City.

came to the United States—mainly to work on building transatlantic railroads. In the mid-1800s, Japan experienced an economic depression, and farmers were heavily taxed to pay for the country's modernization. Many who fell into poverty planned to regain their wealth by earning money abroad as sojourners—temporary immigrants who intended to make money and return home. Also in the mid-1800s, news of the discovery of gold in California reached China. Chinese immigrants and sojourners streamed across the Pacific.

IRISH IMMIGRANTS IN THE NINETEENTH CENTURY

From 1820 to 1870, almost 7.5 million newcomers entered the United States. Nearly all of them came from

These emigrants are preparing to leave County Kerry, Ireland, for the United States. Their baggage is being loaded onto the mail coach.

northern and western Europe. In the early 1800s, Ireland, with a population of 8 million, was the most densely populated country in Europe. Many Irish peasants earned a meager living by raising potatoes on small farms that produced little income, or they leased land on estates and had to pay high rents. Between 1845 and 1847, conditions worsened when potato crop failures—due to diseased plants—caused widespread famine. Between 1846 and 1851, nearly a million Irish died of starvation and disease.[13]

The potato famine and economic conditions in Ireland drove many Irish to the United States. Between 1841 and 1860, 1.7 million Irish immigrants arrived.

By 1870, 4.7 million Irish had made their homes in the United States, a number equal to the total population of Ireland during the 1970s.[14]

Although America offered free or cheap land for farming, most Irish immigrants settled in large, eastern seaboard cities, especially New York and Boston, creating huge ethnic ghettos.[15] Life in America for these immigrants, while no doubt better than what they had left behind, was still harsh. The newcomers faced hostility and prejudice from native-born Americans, many of whom viewed the Irish as "filthy, bad-tempered, and given to drink."[16] Furthermore, employment signs that read "No Irish Need Apply" taunted the new immigrants. The predominantly Protestant culture of the United States also rebuffed the efforts of Irish Catholics to establish separate Catholic schools for their children. Many Protestants saw this effort as an unwillingness on the part of the Irish to let their children become Americanized.

Employment for most Irish immigrants consisted of hard physical labor. Irish women worked mainly in garment factories. Irish men labored to build the Erie Canal, pave roads, and construct railroads. Irish laborers in the South "were sometimes considered more expendable than slaves and were hired at pitifully low wages for the dirtiest and most dangerous jobs, such as clearing snake-infested swamps."[17]

Although Irish immigrants usually held difficult, low-paying jobs, opponents of immigration voiced concern about the effects of immigration on the jobs and wages of native-born Americans. In the 1840s and 1850s, a nativist movement grew out of the anti-immigration mood. The American Protective Association protested Irish immigration. In New York City, the Nativist Party published a newspaper called *Spirit of Seventy-Six.*

The Nativists led to the formation of the American Party, also called the Know-Nothing Party. The American Party was a secret organization as well as a political movement that resisted Roman Catholic immigration in particular and any immigration in general.[18] The Know-Nothings advocated waiting 21 years before immigrants could become naturalized citizens. It was the only Nativist Party to win substantial, widespread power in state and national elections.

The American Party established branches in every county in the states of New York and New Jersey, and

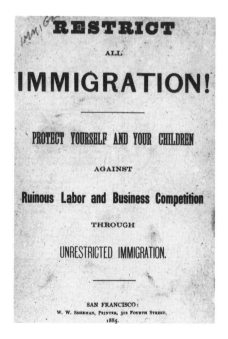

The Know-Nothing Party, also known as the American Party, wanted laws to reduce immigration.

in the cities of Boston, Massachusetts, and Charleston, South Carolina. The party then changed its name to the Native American Party and established a program of anti-foreignism and anti-Catholicism as well as positive reform.

GERMAN IMMIGRANTS IN THE NINETEENTH CENTURY

At the same time that Irish immigrants were arriving, German immigrants were also settling in the United States. By 1860, 1.5 million Germans had made their homes in America.[19]

Unlike the Irish, who were fleeing poverty and famine, the Germans were escaping political unrest. In the mid-1800s, Germany was not a single country. The area was made up of a confederation of states. Efforts to unify the separate states into one German nation were failing. The resulting political turmoil, which included rebellion and several short wars, speeded German immigration to America.[20]

Some German immigrants settled along the eastern seaboard, but large numbers of them also spread throughout the Midwest and Southwest to establish farming communities. So many German-speaking immigrants settled in Texas that a German edition of Texas law was published in 1843.[21] Many towns such as New Braunfels in Texas, Hermann in Missouri, and New Ulm in Minnesota, are named after towns in Germany and can trace their heritage to these early German settlers.

As with the Irish, anti-immigrant hostility was also directed at German immigrants. A hundred years after

Henry J. Heinz, a descendant of German immigrants, liked to personally visit his workers to urge them on to greater productivity. He began to raise and distribute his own vegetables at the age of 16 and went on to found the company that makes Heinz's "57 varieties."

Benjamin Franklin grumbled about German immigrants "swarming" into Pennsylvania and refusing to become "Americanized," the language barrier was still a sore spot with many native-born Americans. Because German immigrants tended to band together in German-speaking enclaves, they were often perceived as clannish by their English-speaking neighbors. Religious and economic factors also affected German immigrants. The Germans, like the Irish, were predominantly Catholic. The nativists, especially the Know-Nothings, argued that America's republican form of government could not endure if too many citizens owed allegiance to the pope (the head of the Roman Catholic Church).

In spite of hardship, criticism, and even hostility, these early immigrants persevered and ultimately became interwoven into the fabric of America. In *Time*

magazine, author John Elson wrote, "The nativist sentiment that foreigners are somehow inferior to the American-born may be the nation's oldest and most
persistent bias."[22]

CHINESE AND JAPANESE IMMIGRANTS IN THE NINETEENTH CENTURY

The first Chinese immigrants arrived in California during the 1840s, most seeking to escape the turmoil of the
Opium War in their own land. The Opium War was a
conflict between Great Britain and China that took
place during the mid-1800s. The conflict was begun by
the British in an effort to end trade restrictions imposed by China. In 1839, the Chinese government
banned the importation of opium, a habit-forming nar-
cotic, and destroyed British-owned opium stored in the
city of Canton.[23] This act launched the war.

Initially, Chinese immigrants were welcomed in the
United States. By 1860, about 24,000 Chinese were
working in California's gold fields. As the Gold Rush—
and the economy—faltered, however, hostility against
the Chinese immigrants began to rise. Many Chinese
miners were hired to build the Central Pacific Railroad
or to dig irrigation canals in the Salinas and San
Joaquin Valleys of California. But their wages were
only two-thirds of what white workers earned.

Unlike European immigrants during the same period, the Chinese had no hope of ever becoming United
States citizens. The 1790 federal Naturalization Law
limited the privilege of citizenship to whites.[24]

Although their numbers were small in comparison to
those of European immigrants, hostility toward people

These Chinese immigrants were hired in 1852 to help mine gold at the Auburn Ravine in California. At that time, U.S. law did not allow them to become naturalized citizens.

The First Article of the Fourteenth Amendment to the U.S. Constitution

All persons born or naturalized in the United States, and subject to the jurisdiction thereof, are citizens of the United States and of the state wherein they reside. No state shall make any law which shall abridge the privileges or immunities of citizens of the United States; nor shall any state deprive any person of life, liberty, or property without due process of law; nor deny to any person within its jurisdiction equal protection of the laws.

of Asian descent increased. This hostility led to the Chinese Exclusion Act of 1882. The new law, enacted by Congress, barred most Chinese workers from entering the United States, although teachers, diplomats, and merchants were allowed in. (The law was extended indefinitely in 1902 and remained in effect for a total of 61 years.)

Following the exclusion of Chinese laborers in 1882, employers turned to Japan as a source of cheap, temporary labor. Between 1885 and 1907, about 157,000 Japanese contract workers immigrated to the sugarcane fields of Hawaii, which officially became a possession of the United States in 1898, and to California.[25]

But Japanese immigrants also became the target of nativism and racism. In 1906, the San Francisco, California, school board ordered that Japanese children be taught in segregated classes. The Japanese government objected, and President Theodore Roosevelt called the

Violent anti-Chinese riots occurred in many western towns during the 1870s and 1880s. This one took place in Denver, Colorado, in 1880.

move "a wicked absurdity," convincing the board to reverse its ruling. California also passed a law aimed at preventing intermarriage between Caucasians and Japanese. In 1907, the Imperial government of Japan agreed to impose limitations on Japanese emigration rather than suffer an exclusion law such as that imposed on the Chinese. That agreement ended immigration of Japanese laborers to the United States. [26]

Two groups of Japanese remained in the United States, however. The Issei, Japanese immigrants who were legal residents, were allowed to stay in the country, but they were barred from citizenship because of their race. The Nisei, American-born children of immigrants, were automatically U.S. citizens because of the Fourteenth Amendment. As citizens, the Nisei had the right to own property and to vote.

THE GOLDEN DOOR SWINGS OPEN: 1890–1920
In 1884, the Statue of Liberty was presented to the United States by the French people as an expression of friendship and of the ideal of liberty shared by both countries. The statue, with its beacon of light, soon welcomed a great wave of new immigrants. Between 1890 and 1920, 12 million new immigrants arrived in the United States. Approximately 100 million Americans—about 40 percent of the U.S. population—trace their heritage to someone who was greeted by the Statue of Liberty and processed into the United States through Ellis Island in New York Harbor.[27]

The government began using Ellis Island as an immigration station in 1892. There, immigrants waited in long lines to be questioned by government officials and

The wood engraving (top) *shows a scene on the steerage deck of an ocean steamer passing the Statue of Liberty. Ellis Island* (bottom) *in New York Harbor was the chief U.S. reception center for immigrants from 1892 to 1924.*

examined by doctors. These new immigrants came
from Italy, Russia, Ukraine, Lithuania, Latvia, Poland,
Serbia, Bohemia, Slovakia, Croatia, Hungary, Greece,
Syria, Spain, and Portugal.[28]

Most immigrants left their homelands to escape
poverty or persecution. During the late nineteenth century and early twentieth century, Russian Jews were
subjected to pogroms—acts of violence against Jewish
communities during which synagogues, homes, businesses, and schools were destroyed. Nearly 2 million
Jews fled Russia and eastern Europe between 1892 and
1907. About 70 percent of them came from Russia.[29]

Many new immigrants found living conditions in the
United States only a little better than those they had left
behind. They lived in cramped apartments in urban
ghettos and worked at menial jobs. Immigrants did the
backbreaking work of constructing railroads, paving
streets, cutting stones, and mining coal. In his book
American Immigration, author Gerald Leinwand, noted:

> Those who came to America expecting quick
> riches were doomed to disappointment. In Swe-
> den, farm workers earned $33.50 a year plus room
> and board. Little wonder that a salary of $40.00 a
> month in a coal mine, or $200.00 a year as a farm-
> hand, was appealing. These figures by themselves
> do not tell the harsh desolation of the often storm-
> swept plains of Kansas, Nebraska, Minnesota, and
> the Dakotas. They do not tell of the squalid condi-
> tions in factories where the immigrants worked
> and slums in which they lived, nor do they speak
> of the labor unions that resented the newcomers'
> presence and often refused them membership. But
> despite the hardships, most immigrants suc-
> ceeded in America.[30]

Immigrants often lived in overcrowded conditions in the bustling streets and the cramped tenements.

THE GOLDEN DOOR SLAMS SHUT: 1921–1965

While these new immigrants were establishing their American roots, anti-immigration forces were working to halt immigration. Opposition to the new wave of immigrants was based on economics and the popular notion that recent immigrants were somehow inferior to people already living in the United States. As early as the 1890s, labor leaders such as Samuel Gompers of the American Federation of Labor called for a halt to unrestricted immigration. Gompers, a Dutch-born Jew who migrated to the United States from England in 1863, complained that the new immigrants were largely "cheap labor, ignorant labor that takes our jobs and cuts our wages."[31]

In 1894, the Boston-based Immigration Restriction League urged Congress to pass a law requiring that all

Samuel Gompers, head of the American Federation of Labor, was a Dutch-born Jew. Nevertheless, he feared that new immigrants threatened American jobs and wages.

Hungarian immigrants Andrew and Elizabeth Tapa showed an intense interest in the American way of life after arriving at La Guardia Airport in New York.

immigrants be literate—able to read and write, preferably in English. New Hampshire author and poet Thomas Bailey Aldrich, an anti-immigration activist, commented at the time that the Immigration Restriction League wanted laws against "accents of menace alien to our air."[32] What really concerned the Immigration Restriction League and other nativists, however, was that the flood of immigrants from Italy, Russia, and eastern European countries might soon outnumber Americans of western European and English origin.[33]

In 1907, President Theodore Roosevelt appointed a congressional Immigration Commission to study the problem. After spending three years and more than a million dollars, the commission issued a 41-volume report. According to the report, the new immigrants were "inferior" to those who had come earlier; the new immigrants did not assimilate well (that is, they hadn't become "Americanized"); and the presence of this great throng of immigrants caused a decrease in wages and job opportunities for native-born Americans.[34]

In 1921, Congress limited the number of immigrants from any single country to 3 percent of the foreign-born people of that nationality living in the United States in 1910. However, no limits were placed on immigrants from Western Hemisphere countries.[35]

The Johnson-Reed Act of 1924 reduced immigration even more drastically. Only 165,000 new immigrants (plus wives, parents, and minor children) were allowed annually, and a quota for each nation was set at 2 percent of the 1890 foreign-born population. Basing the quota on the 1890 census gave preference to immigrants from northern and western Europe.[36]

The National Origins Act of 1929 set American immigration policy until 1965. This legislation allowed only 150,000 immigrants annually. Rather than providing a fixed quota based on each nation, the National Origins Act established a quota for each nationality in proportion to its percentage of the general population of the United States in 1920.

Furthermore, the law required prospective immigrants to obtain a visa from an American consul in the country from which they wished to emigrate. A visa is an official document allowing an individual to remain in a foreign country for a specified length of time. This requirement made it possible for immigration authorities to screen and select potential immigrants.

With strict immigration policies in place and the

Great Depression of the 1930s paralyzing the economy, only about 500,000 immigrants arrived in the United States between 1930 and 1939, as compared to 6 million in each of the two previous decades.[37]

During World War II (1939–1945), immigration to the United States came to a virtual standstill. The War Brides Act of 1945 allowed entry to about 120,000 wives and children of U.S. servicemen who had married while overseas. The Displaced Persons Acts of

A mound of baggage represented the dismantled households of Japanese Americans forced out of their homes during World War II. These San Francisco residents were removed to relocation camps on April 29, 1942.

Over the years, many immigrants have brought valuable technical skills to the United States.

1948 and 1950 allowed another 416,000 refugees from war-torn Europe to settle in the United States.[38] However, American politics became very conservative in the years immediately following World War II. Americans developed a growing fear of the Communist Soviet Union and of Communist sympathizers in the United States. The Internal Security Act of 1950 greatly increased the power of the government to exclude and deport aliens who were considered potentially dangerous to U.S. national security.

In 1952, Congress passed the McCarran-Walter Act, also called the Immigration and Nationality Act, which further restricted immigration—especially to eastern Europeans who might have had Communist ties. This law consolidated all the existing immigration laws into one piece of legislation, but it also established a limit of 160,000 immigrants per year from countries in eastern Europe. The countries of northern and western Europe filled more than 85 percent of the total annual quota. The Act established a system of preference categories that determined which immigrants would be allowed to enter the United States. Between 1953 and 1957, Congress allowed refugees from Communist-dominated countries such as Hungary and Poland to enter the United States. However, these immigrants were counted against future quota allocations.[39]

At the same time, the McCarran-Walter Act opened the door to modest immigration from China and Japan and established special preference categories for immigrants with advanced education, technical skills, and other desirable qualities.[40] Between 1956 and 1965, America acquired 7,000 chemists, 35,000 engineers, 38,000 nurses, and 18,000 physicians. In all, about 2.5 million immigrants arrived in the United States during the 1950s.

THE GOLDEN DOOR CREAKS OPEN: 1965–PRESENT

In 1963, President John F. Kennedy sent an immigration reform bill to Congress. Kennedy, a descendant of Irish immigrants, wanted to repeal the national origins quota system. Kennedy was assassinated in 1963, before he could see an immigration bill enacted into law, but President Lyndon B. Johnson supported Kennedy's immigration policies.

The Hart-Celler Act of 1965 eliminated quotas based on nationality and established new quotas designed to achieve three primary goals: reunite families, open

America's door to refugees, and attract skilled and talented people. The Act set a limit of 290,000 immigrants annually, 170,000 from the Eastern Hemisphere and 120,000 from the Western Hemisphere.

Seven "preference quotas" were established, with first and second preference (40 percent) going to unmarried sons and daughters of citizens and legally admitted alien residents. The third preference (10 percent) was reserved for members of the professions, scientists, and artists. Adult married children of United States citizens also received 10 percent of the allocation. The fifth preference (24 percent) was given to brothers and sisters of citizens. The sixth (10 percent) was reserved for skilled labor, or common laborers in short supply. The final preference (6 percent) was reserved for specifically defined refugees. [41]

When President Johnson signed the 1965 legislation into law, he said the new law "repairs a deep and painful flaw in the fabric of American life. . . . The days of unlimited immigration are past. But those who come will come because of what they are—not because of the land from which they sprung."[42]

What Johnson and the authors of the 1965 Act could not have foreseen was the chaotic shift in the demographics (national origin and social and economic status) of the future immigrants. For example, in 1975 the fall of South Vietnam and Cambodia to Communist North Vietnam caused thousands of refugees, for whom the United States took responsibility, to flee to safety. (The United States entered the Vietnam War in 1961 and ultimately withdrew its forces in 1973.) Within six months after Cambodia fell, the United

In a scene reminiscent of the Mekong Delta, two Vietnamese women haggle over the price of fish in the Michoud area of New Orleans, Louisiana. About 4,000 Vietnamese refugees live in that area of the city.

States had admitted 130,000 Vietnamese and Cambodians under special quota exemptions. By 1990, nearly 600,000 Indo-Chinese refugees made their homes in the United States.[43] Meanwhile, European immigration declined to only about 10 percent between 1965 and 1990. During that same period, however, immigration from Asia, Latin America, Indochina, the Middle East, and Africa steadily increased.

In 1978, hemispheric limits were abolished. A worldwide limit of 290,000 immigrants per year—with no more than 20,000 per country—was established. Between 1981 and 1990, about 7.3 million legal immigrants arrived in the United States. Out of that number, only 761,500 came from Europe, while 3.7 million came from Latin America and another 2.7 million from Asia. The leading contributors of new immigrants were Mexico, with 1,656,000; the Philippines, with 549,000; Vietnam, with 281,000; the People's Republic of China and Taiwan, with 98,000 and 346,000 respectively; and Korea, with 334,000.

At the same time, 872,000 immigrants arrived in the United States from the Caribbean nations; 250,000 from India; 112,000 from Laos; 116,000 from Iran; 468,000 from the Central American countries of Costa Rica, El Salvador, Guatemala, Honduras, Nicaragua,

Sikhs belong to one of the religions of India. These Sikh immigrants marched in a demonstration in New York City.

and Panama; and 177,000 from various African nations.[44]

The first major modification to the 1965 law occurred in 1980, when President Jimmy Carter signed the Refugee Act into law. According to the 1980 law, a refugee is anyone who could not remain in his or her own country by reason of a "well-founded fear of persecution" on the basis of race, religion, nationality, or political opinion. The 1980 law eliminated the 1965 seventh preference (a refugee quota of 17,400 annually) and allowed an annual quota of up to 50,000 refugees, or more if they could be admitted for "grave, humanitarian reasons." At the same time, the quota for other immigrants was dropped from 290,000 to 270,000 per year.[45] Indeed, many new nationalities were added to the melting pot.

A member of the Border Patrol searched an illegal alien in Laredo, Texas, before loading him into a bus that will carry him back to Mexico.

IMMIGRATION POLICY

The Immigration and Naturalization Service, a branch of the U.S. Justice Department, is in charge of enforcing immigration law. The INS oversees the Border Patrol, which was established by Congress in 1924. The Border Patrol was originally created to stop the smuggling of illegal aliens by boat to states along the Gulf of Mexico. In 1925, the patrol was expanded to cover land borders as well. The purpose of the Border Patrol is to ensure that no one enters the United States without following proper procedures. The patrol apprehends many of those who attempt or manage to do so. Patrol agents also operate entry posts on all highways leading into the United States, and they are responsible for intercepting contraband—illegal items such as weapons or drugs.

Anyone who wants to immigrate legally to the United States must first apply to the State Department for an immigration visa, an official document that allows the applicant to enter the country. Immigrants may legally enter the United States provided

- they have job skills desired here, or
- they have relatives who are United States citizens, or
- they are refugees from war or are seeking political asylum to escape persecution in their own countries.

People living in the United States without authorization from the government are considered illegal aliens.

RECENT IMMIGRATION LEGISLATION

In September 1996, Congress enacted two separate pieces of legislation, each of which will have a significant effect on immigrants. One of the laws, the Immigration Reform Bill of 1996, left legal immigration quotas as they were, but made it more expensive for legal immigrants or immigrants who have become U.S. citizens to sponsor family members who want to immigrate to the United States. The Immigration Reform Bill also provided funds to double the size of the United States Border Patrol within five years and assured swift deportation for those caught entering the United States illegally. The bill also authorized $12 million for additional Border Patrol equipment and technology, including a 14-mile-long border fence south of San Diego, California. That provision of the bill allowed the U.S. attorney general to waive environmental protection laws for construction of the fence—a move that drew angry protests from environmentalists and ecologists.

A second law, the federal Welfare Reform Bill of 1996, put restrictions on many federal benefits, such as food stamps and Supplemental Security Income (SSI, a cash benefit for the elderly and disabled), to legal

The Welfare Reform Bill of 1996

- Legal immigrants who are not U.S. military veterans or have not worked and paid taxes in the United States for at least 10 years are prohibited from any Supplemental Security Income or food stamp benefits.
- Legal immigrants who arrived after August 22, 1996, are prohibited from receiving most federal benefits during their first five years in the country.
- After the five-year ban, new immigrants who have sponsors must include their sponsor's income when applying for federal benefits.
- Students are eligible for school lunch programs as long as they are legally eligible for free public education.
- Illegal immigrants are ineligible for federal, state, and local public benefits.[1]

immigrants. The bill also denied benefits to all illegal immigrants.

The Welfare Reform Bill cut spending on food stamps by 14 percent, or $27 billion over six years. Among the hardest hit by the new laws were legal immigrants, who were no longer eligible for food stamps or Supplemental Security Income during their first 10 years in the United States.

Republican sponsors of the Welfare Reform Bill argued that the cost of food stamps, the nation's largest welfare program, had spiraled out of control. At the time the bill was signed into law, food stamps were being used by 27 million people—one out of every ten. Congressman Pat Roberts, a Kansas Republican, said, "We wanted to take the program off the automatic spending pilot." [3]

Opponents of the bill, such as Robert Greenstein, executive director of the Washington-based Center on Budget and Policy Priorities, feared the new legislation would only serve to increase hunger in already poor communities. "Cuts of this magnitude are unprecedented," Greenstein said. "Not even during the early years of the Reagan administration [1981–1989] have there ever been cuts approaching these in depth and breadth. They will affect every poor family and every individual on food stamps."[4] Officials estimated that about 900,000 legal immigrants would lose food stamps under the new law and another 350,000 elderly or disabled immigrants would lose Supplemental Security Income benefits.[5]

The Immigration Reform Bill was even more controversial. Debate about the bill began in mid-1995. One proposed amendment to the bill would have banned the children of illegal immigrants from attending public schools. The amendment was sponsored by Republican congressman Elton Gallegly of California, who saw the measure as a way to fight illegal immigration.

Opponents of Gallegly's amendment argued that the provision would punish children rather than their parents, who had made the decision to enter the country illegally. Children of illegal aliens had been allowed to attend public schools, and these children, as well as their illegal immigrant parents, had been entitled to emergency medical care. Gallegly's amendment was withdrawn a short time before President Clinton signed the bill into law.

Another proposed amendment also drew fire from immigration advocates. This proposal would have

The Immigration Reform Bill of 1996
- No more than 675,000 legal immigrants are allowed to enter the United States annually. (This figure remains the same as in the 1990 legislation.)
- Approximately 100,000 refugees are allowed to enter the United States each year. (According to Carlos Angulo, legislative aide to Senator Paul Simon, this figure may fluctuate and will be reviewed annually.)[2]
- Eligible relatives of residing legal immigrants are defined as parents, children, siblings (brothers and sisters), and spouses of siblings.
- Legal immigrants or citizens wishing to sponsor a foreign relative must have a household income equal to 125 percent of the poverty level. A family of four would need a household income of $19,500 annually (the poverty level of $15,600 for a family of four, plus $3,900). The income requirement would assure INS authorities that the sponsoring family would be able to support a legal immigrant until the new arrival became self-sufficient.
- Funds are provided to increase the size of the Border Patrol by 5,000 new agents over the next five years, thereby doubling the size of the force.
- An expenditure of $12 million is authorized for new Border Patrol equipment and the construction of a 14-mile-long border fence south of San Diego, California.

given the Immigration and Naturalization Service the power to deport any legal immigrants who used more than one year's worth of government services, including subsidized housing and child care, during their first seven years of residency.[6] Supporters of the provision, such as Republican congressman Lamar Smith of Texas, argued that the incentive of government benefits is abused by legal and illegal immigrants alike. "We will continue to keep the welcome mat out. We just are not going to be a doormat anymore," Smith commented.[7]

Opponents of the proposed amendment claimed the measure unfairly targeted legal immigrants. Senator Edward Kennedy, a Democrat from Massachusetts, said, "This bill does more to hurt American citizens and legal immigrants than it does to stop illegal immigration."[8] Democratic Senator Paul Simon of Illinois called the measure "deeply flawed."[9] The deportation proposal was removed before Congress passed the Immigration Reform Bill.

NATURALIZATION: BECOMING A UNITED STATES CITIZEN

All immigrants must possess an Alien Registration Card, a form of identification issued to legal immigrants by the INS. The registration card is more commonly called a "green card." The green card has no time restrictions and allows an immigrant to legally live and work in the United States.

At the Atlanta Civic Center, 1,200 immigrants from 80 nations were sworn in as U.S. citizens during the largest naturalization ceremony ever performed in Georgia.

To apply for citizenship, an immigrant must be at least 18 years old and must have been a resident of the United States for at least 5 years. An immigrant seeking naturalization must also be proficient in English, unless he or she is over 50 years old and has been a legal resident for 20 years or more.

The naturalization process begins with an application to the INS. The application includes fingerprints and background information including criminal history, if any. With two citizens present as witnesses, the applicant offers proof of age, residence, character, and education, then takes written and oral tests to demonstrate a basic understanding of United States history and government. Later, at a final hearing, a judge reviews the process, listens to the recommendations of an INS officer, and decides whether to grant citizenship. If the applicant is approved, he or she is then sworn in as a new United States citizen.

In the past, applicants had a waiting period (about a year and a half) before a naturalization exam was

A teacher discussed the meaning of July 4th with a class of Soviet immigrants during an English class. The two most popular questions were: What is a barbecue and did Lincoln sign the Declaration of Independence.

scheduled. In 1995, however, the Clinton administration launched a $77 million Citizenship USA program aimed at eliminating the backlog of 600,000 naturalization applications stuck in the INS processing pipeline.[10] The program features standardized and simplified multiple-choice and written examinations as well as streamlined and simplified oral interview requirements. By October 1996, about 1.3 million immigrants had been granted U.S. citizenship, more than in any other year in American history and almost triple the 459,846 new citizens in 1995.[11]

The Citizenship USA program did not change the basic process of becoming a citizen, but it did eliminate confusion and complications in the testing process, INS officials said. For example, citizenship candidates are given preparation packets that include five sample multiple-choice questions and a list of one hundred possible questions. They also receive a list of vocabulary study words to be used during the actual examination.[12]

The standardized tests can be given to as many as 50 applicants at a time to avoid the possibility of an examiner unfairly choosing questions. Brian Perryman, acting district director of the Chicago INS office, commenting on the new system, said, "We want to take the mystery out of what it means to become a citizen."[13]

Naturalized citizens enjoy the same rights that native-born citizens do, with one exception. A naturalized citizen cannot run for the office of president or vice president of the United States. Otherwise, new citizens may hold any other office, vote, apply for government jobs, and travel freely.

WHAT ABOUT ILLEGAL IMMIGRANTS?

The number of illegal aliens—people living in the United States without authorization from the government—is unknown. One estimate places the number between 300,000 and 500,000 per year. Experts estimate that as many as 3.3 million illegal immigrants live in the United States.[14]

Illegal immigrants can slip into the United States by various means. Many simply run or swim across unguarded portions of the vast United States–Mexico border. Slightly more than half of all illegal immigrants come from Mexico. Others enter United States airports with forged documents or remain in the United States after their tourist or student visas have expired.

Illegal immigrants who are caught are subject to automatic deportation, but typically, once in the United States, they blend easily into ethnic communities, find work, and stay on as undocumented workers. Nearly all come to work and save money. Although some illegal immigrants find good jobs, most have jobs with low pay, long hours, and harsh conditions. Some workers are abused or cheated by their employers. But even in low-paying jobs, illegal workers can earn more than they could in their own country.

Illegal immigrants have no real "rights" under United States law, but they are still entitled to emergency medical care, and their children are allowed to attend public schools. And, according to the Fourteenth Amendment of the Constitution, any child born on United States soil, no matter the legal status of the parents, is automatically a United States citizen.

EFFORTS TO REPEAL OR REVISE THE FOURTEENTH AMENDMENT

Although the issue may never be considered by Congress, some people would like to repeal or revise the Fourteenth Amendment. This movement began in 1993, just before California voters approved Proposition 187, a measure that would deny basic medical care to all illegal immigrants and public schooling to children of illegal immigrants.

Judy Mark, communications coordinator for the National Immigration Forum in Washington, D.C., said the movement is not highly organized, but it has been endorsed by numerous anti-immigration forces, especially in states where illegal immigration is a major

A special agent
views forged
documents
confiscated from
illegal aliens in
New York (top).
Migrant workers
from Mexico are
hired to pick
cucumbers
(bottom).

problem. Mark said opposition to the Fourteenth
Amendment is primarily rhetorical (talk) and that no
bills have yet been introduced in Congress.[15]

Nevertheless, Representative Bill McCollum, a
Florida Republican, was successful in introducing a

Fourteenth Amendment revision plank in the Republican Party platform during the party's 1996 national convention.

Karl Kaufmann, legislative director for Representative McCollum, said the goal is not so much to repeal, but to clarify the Fourteenth Amendment. Kaufmann said McCollum and other supporters of the Fourteenth Amendment revision believe the original intent of the amendment has been distorted by current immigration laws. When the Fourteenth Amendment was first drafted, Kaufmann said, there were no immigration laws and no illegal immigrants. The intent of the Fourteenth Amendment, he said, was to grant citizenship to and prevent discrimination against former slaves.

What Fourteenth Amendment opponents hope to do, Kaufmann said, is end birthright citizenship to the children of illegal immigrants. "People come here illegally," Kaufmann said. "They run across the border, give birth, and suddenly, that child is a citizen, and eligible for all sorts of benefits. Children of illegal aliens should be considered aliens as well. They should not be considered citizens simply because their parents were successful at evading U.S. law."[16]

While the Fourteenth Amendment repeal or revision movement may have drawn support from many anti-immigration forces, it concerns people like Juan José Gutierrez, a Latino-American labor rights activist from Seattle, Washington. "Thousands of Americans died fighting the Civil War," Gutierrez said at a "Welfare Reform–Impact on Immigrant Communities" workshop in Seattle in 1994. "From their blood sacrifice came the Fourteenth Amendment, which gives Americans the birthright of citizenship—a person born on American soil is a citizen. Now . . . Americans are seeking to repeal that concept, all to harass immigrants."[17]

Gutierrez said that he and others who oppose the repeal movement fear that the present anti-immigration mood could lead to a "national citizenship card," as proposed by some who support the movement. Every citizen would be required to carry such a card and produce it upon demand to prove his or her citizenship. In that case, Gutierrez explained, any state or federal agency could immediately determine the citizenship status of anyone and give or deny that person benefits. "Eventually, people would be required to drag this document around just to sign their children up for Little League, enroll in public schools, or apply for medical assistance," Gutierrez said.[18]

New federal legislation regarding immigrants is in place, at least for the moment. But it is highly unlikely that public and political debate concerning immigrants, especially illegal immigrants, will subside in the foreseeable future.

Illegal Mexican immigrants leap into the United States from a fence that divides California and an area of Mexico near Tijuana.

CRISIS IN CALIFORNIA

Since the 1970s, California's population has grown rapidly, in part because of large numbers of immigrants from Europe, Asia, and especially Central America and Mexico. In 1986, California voters approved a measure to make English the state's official language. In 1994, voters passed Proposition 187—a measure to prohibit illegal immigrants from receiving public education, medical care, and other social services. Several lawsuits were filed against the proposition, however.

Slightly more than a year after Proposition 187 was approved by 60 percent of California voters, U.S. District Court Judge Mariana Pfaelzer declared most of the proposed legislation unconstitutional.[1] Had Proposition 187 become law, it would have denied free public education to the children of illegal immigrants, barred illegal immigrants from receiving federally funded medical care, and required that health care personnel, police officers, and educators report anyone suspected of being in violation of immigration law. Pfaelzer did allow one provision of Proposition 187, however. She upheld new criminal penalties for the sale and use of false immigration documents.[2]

A *Chicago Tribune* editorial concluded, "The judge said that the verification and reporting requirements invaded the sovereign territory of the federal government, which has authority over immigration. Supporters of the initiative wouldn't necessarily disagree in principle, but they feel Washington has abrogated [ignored] its responsibility to police the borders and enforce the law—leaving California a perpetual headache and expense."[3]

The ruling of Judge Pfaelzer may have put Proposition 187 to rest temporarily, but certainly not the controversy that prompted it and made it a nationwide

Activists for and against Proposition 187 were separated by a police line during a rally in Los Angeles in August 1994. The proposition was approved by California voters in November 1994 but was later declared unconstitutional in a U.S. district court.

issue. Californians no doubt feel they have a legitimate gripe concerning immigration. According to statistics, this state has absorbed nearly 3 million of the 9 million legal immigrants new to this country in the past decade. About 2 million illegal immigrants have entered the state during the same period.[4]

The city of Santa Ana, California, has become the second-most Latino city in the United States (after El Paso, Texas). Nearly 70 percent of its 600,000 residents are recent immigrants from Mexico and Central America.[5] Ron Heike, a corporate sales manager, moved to Santa Ana over 20 years ago and "found a suburban, middle-class neighborhood of his dreams."[6] Heike is angry and concerned about problems he and many other Californians feel are a direct result of uncontrolled immigration.

In a 1993 interview with writer William McGowan, Heike pointed to trash-littered streets, overcrowded housing, and groups of day laborers milling about in parking lots, waiting to be hired. "We have to stop that kind of stuff," Heike told McGowan. "How we do it we are not certain yet. [But] more intrusions like this and this neighborhood is going to go."[7]

It would be irresponsible as well as untrue to suggest that immigrants, legal or illegal, are any more likely than anyone else to throw trash in the streets. But this isolated instance in Santa Ana, California, serves to illustrate just one of many elements that have fueled the nativist mood in that state.

Adding fuel to the fires of anti-immigration sentiment was California's recent economic downturn. In 1993, the state lost 500,000 jobs and held the dubious

Suspected illegal immigrants await transport from a house raided by the Immigration and Naturalization Service in Bell Gardens, California. During the raid, 54 suspected illegal immigrants and 5 suspected smugglers were arrested.

honor of boasting a 10 percent unemployment rate—3 percentage points higher than the national average at the time.[8] By 1996, the economic situation had improved somewhat, although unemployment remained high—10.9 percent in Los Angeles and 10 percent in Oakland. Los Angeles had a Hispanic population of 39.9 percent, while in Oakland the Hispanic population totaled only 13.9 percent.[9] In San Jose, with 26.6 percent of the population being Hispanic, the 1996 unemployment figure was 8 percent.[10]

People tend to blame others, either for individual problems or for problems affecting the population as a whole. In 1993, McGowan noted, "Many [California] natives are blaming immigrants for the decline. And a fierce debate has enveloped the state over how many immigrants it can absorb—a debate that might define the terms for the rest of the nation as well."[11]

California's governor, Pete Wilson, has carried the anti-immigration banner nationwide. He has tried "to curb illegal immigration and to confront Washington on what he perceives as inadequate federal funding to halt the flow of illegal immigrants into his state."[12]

In January 1996, Wilson demanded that the federal government pay California's expenses for thousands of criminal illegal aliens housed in the state prisons. According to Wilson, California had more than 20,000 illegal aliens behind bars—five times more than any other state and enough to fill eight state prisons. Wilson and other state officials said the number of illegal

Governor Pete Wilson of California led a nationwide rally against immigration.

alien felons (people convicted of serious crimes) had more than tripled during the previous seven years, and so had the cost of imprisoning them. Wilson estimated that it cost California $491 million a year to imprison illegal aliens convicted of crimes.[13]

ONGOING DEBATE

Other Californians, such as Bill Hughes, who writes for the *Oakland Post*, agree with Wilson—but only to a point. "There are such compelling arguments on both sides of the issue," wrote Hughes in a recent editorial. "On one hand we all have to admit that America, in the last analysis, is itself nothing but a nation of immigrants." Hughes then cited the inscription on the base of the Statue of Liberty and asked, "Hey, how can we argue against such a compassionate statement of prin-

Signs along freeways near the U.S.-Mexican border in California try to warn drivers of people crossing the road. Many illegal immigrants who successfully cross the border have never seen high-speed freeways.

A Mexican citizen from Tijuana climbs back to the Mexican side of the fence dividing California and Mexico. The man said he has been unable to enter the United States because of an increased vigilance by the U.S. Border Patrol.

ciple which has stood the nation in good stead for so many years? Did we not accept the waves of immigration of the Irish, the Italians, the Germans, the Jews and the Chinese, even if we did not always do it with open arms? Did we not even force African Americans to come to our shores so we could exploit them? And have not all these people contributed richly to the American culture and the American dream?"[14]

"So why," Hughes questions, "do we now object when hordes of those poor and huddled masses from our good neighbor Mexico cross the border in ever increasing numbers? After all, we sought them out for many years to come across the border and work as impoverished laborers in the building of the agricultural empire in California. And yet, now we tell them to stay home and not bother us. So what's the problem?"[15]

There are several problems, according to Hughes. For example, the conditions in the United States today are not the conditions that prevailed when immigration was encouraged. The population was much smaller then, and growth was necessary to spur the nation's economy. Legal immigrants from Mexico, Hughes suggests, are not the ones who are causing problems. "It is the constant flow of illegal immigrants who are straining the capacity of this country to absorb them into the domestic economy, particularly in California."[16] The biggest problem, according to Hughes, "is deciding where the responsibility of the United States ends and the responsibility of Mexico begins in caring for these 'huddled masses' cited on that tablet in the Statue of Liberty."[17]

One scholar, Gary S. Becker, a 1992 Nobel laureate and a teacher at the University of Chicago, endorsed Proposition 187, but added, "the overwhelming case for tougher policies toward illegal aliens doesn't justify calls for a cutback on all immigration."[18] The problem with illegal aliens, he wrote in a *Business Week* editorial, did not emerge until the past couple of decades, "when travel became cheaper and the desire to immigrate exploded, partly because of the benefits provided by the welfare state." Becker suggests that the United States "will benefit from even larger numbers of [legal] immigrants if illegal entry is curtailed and if young, skilled applicants either directly or indirectly receive top priority."[19]

Meanwhile, various religious leaders have joined together to combat what Rabbi Doug Kahn of San Francisco's Jewish Community Relations Council called "an anti-immigrant hysteria." Kahn said, "There is a concern about the ability of the state to adequately

Although Nobel laureate and University of Chicago professor Gary Becker supported Proposition 187, he thinks the United States would benefit from large numbers of legal immigrants.

address the enormous social issues of education, health and welfare. While we resist any effort to suggest that illegal immigration is the major source of that burden, the fact is that there are costs attached to it."[20]

Kahn said policies such as Proposition 187 should be resisted, but he still called on the state and the federal government to "humanely" curtail the flow of illegals. "If a solution isn't found to deal with illegal immigration," he noted, "it may lead to an erosion of support for sustaining legal immigration."[21]

Although Judge Pfaelzer ruled the bulk of Proposition 187 unconstitutional, her decision has been appealed and may eventually end up in the U. S. Supreme Court. According to *Chicago Tribune* political writer Karen Brandon, "The illegal immigration issue that so charged the 1994 elections is not going away."[22]

A rescuer holds a Chinese illegal alien by his pants as he tries to transfer him from the grounded freighter Golden Venture *to a small boat. The freighter was carrying 200 Chinese, who were trying to enter the United States illegally.*

BOAT AND
BORDER PEOPLE

The Federation for American Immigration Reform
(FAIR) and the National Immigration Forum (NIF) are
two prominent organizations, both based in Washington, D.C. FAIR advocates increased restrictions on immigration. NIF, a coalition of about 150 immigrant
organizations, civil rights organizations, trade unions,
and church and legal groups, is dedicated to "defend-
ing and extending the rights of refugees and immigrants in the United States."[1]

Founded in 1979, FAIR describes itself as a "public
interest organization that seeks to improve border security, stop illegal immigration, and reduce legal immigration through a moratorium." FAIR claims to have
50,000 members nationwide and has branches in
Sacramento, San Diego, and Los Angeles. Its members
believe that "today more immigrants are entering this
country—legally and illegally—than at any time in our
history," a situation FAIR contends is "against the best
interests of the people, economy, and ecology of the
United States."[2]

In 1992, Dan Stein, executive director of FAIR, urged national lawmakers to hire more Border Patrol agents, build walls along portions of the Mexican-American border, consider a mandatory, fraud-proof work permit and driver's license for both citizens and noncitizens, and convert abandoned U.S. military bases to "detention centers for criminal . . . and other aliens."[3] FAIR has proposed limiting total immigration to about 300,000 people per year, but it has also proposed suspending admission of most immigrants indefinitely.

NIF, formerly called the National Immigration, Refugee, and Citizenship Forum, was founded during the 1980s "to fight the tide of xenophobia sweeping across the country."[4] (Xenophobia is an unreasonable fear of foreigners or strangers or of strange or foreign customs.) NIF supports the legal immigration of about 800,000 people annually and opposes any moratorium. But like FAIR, NIF supports improved border controls to reduce illegal immigration. NIF executive director Frank Sharry said, "We agree [with FAIR] that as a sovereign nation, the United States has a right and a duty to control our borders. We disagree over means."[5]

Many politicians, civic organizations, and individuals have chosen sides in the immigration controversy as well. Immersed in the ongoing debate are three important issues that have drawn great public and political attention. These issues are political asylum, social services for immigrants, and bilingual education.

POLITICAL ASYLUM

A tragic event that occurred just a few hundred yards off the coast of New York City in June 1993 called public attention to the issue of immigrants and political asylum. A ship called the *Golden Venture* ran aground in a storm and spilled its cargo of 300 illegal Chinese immigrants into the Atlantic Ocean. Most of the passengers swam the 200 yards to shore, but 10 drowned and 16 were injured. Police and immigration officials arrested the survivors as they made their way to shore.[6]

This incident set off a firestorm of debate as to whether the ill-fated passengers qualified for political asylum or whether they were simply trying to slide past the usual channels of immigration. It was reported at the time that many of the passengers had spent their life savings for passage aboard the ship. The surviving passengers claimed they were indeed being oppressed

These Chinese illegal aliens are wrapped in blankets while they huddle on a beach in the Rockaway section of New York City after the Golden Venture *ran aground in the predawn hours on June 6, 1993.*

and persecuted in their homeland. They cited China's alleged abuse of human rights and lack of political freedom. Moreover, they claimed, they had left China illegally and would be imprisoned if they were returned. Many immigration advocates said the United States should accept the *Golden Venture* passengers, if only to atone for the Chinese Exclusion Act. Others argued that the passengers had come here for economic reasons, not political ones, and that they should be sent back to China to apply for legal entry into the United States.

The *Golden Venture* incident also touched off two other topics of debate. First, what exactly constitutes "political persecution" as a valid reason for asylum?

Chinese illegal aliens from the Golden Venture were escorted to buses from the Immigration and Naturalization Service. They were sent to INS detention centers in Pennsylvania.

The second topic related to organized smuggling of illegal immigrants into the United States. Immigration officials learned that the *Golden Venture* was part of an elaborate smuggling ring operated by Chinese gangs, called "snakeheads." Smuggling Chinese immigrants into the United States is estimated to be a $3-billion-a-year industry in China. Sources say snakeheads often charge fees of $20,000 to $30,000 per person. The operation requires an advance deposit. The balance is collected directly from the illegal immigrant or from the immigrant's family.[7]

America has a long tradition of being a refuge for the oppressed, and the *Golden Venture* incident highlights a current dilemma. How can the United States enforce laws against illegal immigration while safeguarding the civil and human rights of immigrants? Are these people simply illegal immigrants, or are they indeed deserving of refugee status and political asylum?

SOCIAL SERVICES AND IMMIGRANTS

Immigration critics contend that large numbers of immigrants, especially illegal aliens, concentrated in a few urban areas create housing, health, education, unemployment, and crime problems. The majority of illegal immigrants tend to settle in California, New York, Texas, Illinois, and Florida. Los Angeles, San Francisco, San Diego, New York City, Newark, Houston, San Antonio, Chicago, and Miami harbor 200,000 to 500,000 illegal immigrants—perhaps more.[8] Most are poor and lack job skills and education.

Immigration foes in these states say illegal immigrants are bleeding state treasuries at the expense of

Mexican illegal aliens escape from a freight train in an attempt to elude immigration agents. The Border Patrol had stopped the train in Laredo, Texas, to check for aliens heading north. The agents captured 55 aliens.

taxpaying citizens. A 1992 California study reported that illegal immigrants cost Los Angeles County $700 million more in social services than they had paid in taxes.[9] The study showed that two-thirds of the babies born in Los Angeles County hospitals had been delivered free of charge to illegal immigrants, and that 23 percent of the county's welfare caseload consisted of children of illegal aliens. Those children, born on U.S. soil automatically became citizens and were therefore eligible for public aid programs.

At the same time, immigration advocates and civil rights groups believe illegal immigrants should be entitled to many of the same benefits available to citizens —benefits such as housing programs and supplemental income—so that they can more quickly join the labor force and contribute to the U.S. economy.

John O'Sullivan, editor of the conservative magazine *National Review,* believes immigration "fosters and expands constituencies of the poor, who, not unnaturally, favor the extension of welfare programs from which they benefit."[10] Furthermore, O'Sullivan contends, the welfare participation rate among immigrants in 1990 was 9.1 percent, 1.7 percent more than that of Americans as a whole. O'Sullivan also points to skill levels of recent legal immigrants. He notes that only 4 percent are admitted to the United States on the basis of their job skills. This situation, he fears, could lead to a large "underclass" of unskilled immigrants.[11]

David Cole, a professor at Georgetown University Law Center and a volunteer staff attorney for the Center for Constitutional Rights, doesn't agree. In a 1994 article for *The Nation,* Cole attempted to explode what he called "myths" concerning immigration. Cole says immigrants are a net benefit to the economy, and he cites a 1994 Urban Institute report which concluded that "immigrants generate significantly more in taxes paid than they cost in services received,"[12] although he didn't cite actual figures. In 1986, the Council of Economic Advisors similarly reported that "immigrants have a favorable effect on the overall standard of living."[13] Cole argues that illegal immigrants are ineligible for most social programs, except public education, emergency health care, and nutritional assistance to poor women, children, and infants. "To deny such basic care to people in need, apart from being inhumanly callous," he says, "would probably cost us more

This Haitian woman carries her infant child from the U.S. Coast Guard cutter Dallas at Guantanamo Bay Naval Base, where she will be housed in a "tent city" with 2,500 other illegal Haitians.

Many immigrants, such as this electronics technician, bring valuable skills and benefit the U.S. economy.

in the long run by exacerbating [making worse] health problems that we would eventually have to address."[14]

Cole's concerns are reflected in the words of 32-year-old Julie Martinez, a legal immigrant who lives in Rio Grande City, Texas, and shares a one-bedroom mobile home with her four children. "If they take our food stamps away, what can we do?" asked Martinez in an interview with the Associated Press.[15] Martinez was speaking about the 1996 Welfare Reform Bill, which denies food stamps to her because she is not a U.S. citizen. Her children's benefits will continue because they were born in the United States. The family had been receiving about $400 a month in food stamps, but under the new law that amount would be reduced to $300. Martinez, unemployed and separated from her husband, wondered how her family would survive on the lower amount when trying to live on $400 was already difficult. The issue of social services to immigrants, both legal and illegal, is one that will stir controversy and generate debate for a long time to come.

BILINGUAL EDUCATION

Until recently in the United States, you could hear Spanish, Polish, German, French, and many other languages being spoken in neighborhoods, workplaces, and churches, but not in public school classrooms. Traditionally, non-English-speaking immigrants attended public schools where they had to learn English quickly or risk failure. By 1968, however, the "sink or swim" approach began to collapse, and many local school districts, seeking to head off a growing dropout rate, began bilingual education programs. Bilingual education typically provides a curriculum in both English and in the native language of immigrant children.

The goal of bilingual programs is to teach non-English-speaking students the basics in their own language and at the same time slowly expose them to English. Naomi Barber, director of the New Visions Project at Leadership School in New York City, believes that developing skills in a native language leads to a quicker mastery of English. Bilingual programs, she contends, also turn out students who are fluent in two languages, thereby "giving them a competitive edge in America's increasingly diverse society."[16]

Critics such as Bill Anderson, director of government relations at U.S. English, an organization that advocates English as the official language of the United States, disagree. Anderson and others say the bilingual

programs do not produce students who are truly proficient in English. "The original concept of bilingual education," Anderson said, "was to immerse students
into the English language within two to three years.
But schools with bilingual programs are never getting
around to English." Anderson called English "the language of equal opportunity," and added, "the longer
you delay the immersion into the English language, the
more you put that child at a disadvantage."[17]

Critics of bilingual education feel that separate languages threaten the "national identity" of the United
States. John O'Sullivan, himself an Irish immigrant, believes that immigration undermines America's identity

*Until recently, English was the only language used in U.S.
public schools—no matter what country students came from
or what language they spoke.*

Many people believe that preserving ethnic languages and cultures undermines an American identity and creates cultural ghettos.

because "it strengthens and reinforces ethnic subcultures in American society."[18] In an editorial entitled "America's Identity Crises," O'Sullivan wrote, ". . . the arrival of more and more people here speaking a language other than English means, quite simply, that those already here who speak that language will have more opportunity to continue doing so and less incentive to learn English. Cultural ghettos that otherwise would gradually be absorbed into the surrounding culture survive and even expand. That is why Miami is now a largely Spanish-speaking city known as 'the capital of Latin America.'"[19]

Language barriers and bilingual education can also unite immigrants. Consider Cristi Hernandez, who came to Queens, New York, in 1986 at the age of 10, along with her mother and older brother—all illegal immigrants. By age 17, Cristi was a senior at Newtown High School, which boasted the largest program in New York for students learning English as a second language. At the time, three-quarters of Newtown's 4,600 students were immigrants. They came from 73 countries and spoke dozens of different languages. Cristi mastered English, even though she said it was difficult at first. "I couldn't express myself in English and I thought Americans would get bored trying to understand me," she said. "I was alone a lot, depressed, and bitter."[20]

Many people believe that assimilation, especially by way of a common language, is the most important step in preserving American culture. Without the common bond of language, immigration critics fear, the United States will become a vast land of subcultures, each practicing its own language and customs.

Theodore Chavez, a native of the Mexican state of Michoacan, picks cherries in the state of Washington. In recent years, thousands of Mexicans have migrated to the Yakima Valley of central Washington.

IMMIGRANTS AND THE U.S. ECONOMY: JOBS, WELFARE, CRIME

Immigration foes claim that illegal immigrants have taken more than 3.5 million jobs from American workers during the last decade.[1] Immigration advocates argue that illegal immigrants take jobs Americans don't want and help expand our economy by paying for food, housing, and other products.

David Cole argues that "there is virtually no evidence" to support the claim that immigrants take jobs from U.S. citizens.[2] Rather, he says, numerous studies documented by the 1994 American Civil Liberties Union Immigrants' Rights Project report prove that immigrants actually create more jobs than they fill. Immigrants, he contends, are typically "highly productive, often starting their own businesses and employing

85

other immigrants and citizens alike."[3] Cole cites one study that found Mexican immigration to Los Angeles County between 1970 and 1980 created 78,000 new jobs. Whether the study focused on legal or illegal immigrants, or both, is not noted. In New York alone, Cole says, immigrants own more than 40,000 companies, providing thousands of jobs and adding $3.5 billion to the state's economy every year.[4]

Economist Donald Huddle takes the opposite view, however. He argues that immigrants make it more difficult for American citizens to find jobs and that unemployment for citizens who have lost jobs lasts longer because of legal and illegal immigrants.[5] Even the jobs of highly skilled and educated citizens are threatened

An American Civil Liberties Union report contends that immigrants are highly productive and actually create more jobs than they fill.

A study conducted by the Institute of Medicine concluded that foreign-trained medical graduates in residency or fellowship training in the United States rose 80 percent between 1988 and 1993. Three-fourths of those who come for residency training stay to work here.

by immigrants, Huddle contends, noting specifically that immigrants with medical degrees or nursing experience are making it difficult for American doctors and nurses to find positions in hospitals. Professionals and unskilled workers alike are forced to compete with immigrants who are typically willing to work for lower pay, Huddle argues.[6]

Huddle's argument regarding the medical profession is supported by a 1995 study conducted by the Washington, D.C.–based Institute of Medicine, which is funded by the National Academy of Sciences. The study concluded that "a surging number of foreign-trained doctors is causing an oversupply of physicians in the United States, threatening to discourage young, talented Americans from going into medicine."[7] According to the Institute of Medicine, foreign-trained medical graduates in residency or fellowship training in the U.S. rose from 12,433 to 22,706 between 1988 and 1993—an increase of 80 percent. The number of U.S. medical school graduates during the same period remained at about 17,500.[8]

Dr. Neal A. Vanselow, Professor of Medicine at Tulane University, says that 75 percent of international medical graduates who come to the United States for residency training stay here to practice.[9] A resident is a doctor who is employed full-time by a hospital for a specified period of time, usually to gain advanced training in a particular field of medicine. This situation, according to Vanselow, "decreases the opportunity for talented young persons from this country to enter the medical profession and may deprive other countries of the services of their own youth."[10]

Immigration critics say immigrant workers are also taking entry-level jobs away from U.S. citizens who need them most: the poor, minorities, and women. Even more jobs are lost when well-paid factory workers are replaced by illegal immigrants who are willing to work in low-paying sweatshops.[11]

Of course, there are innumerable factories and shops, union and nonunion alike that offer decent wages, safe working conditions, and benefits to their employees. Still, as pointed out by writer Ken Silverstein, there are employers who take advantage of newcomers, especially illegal immigrants. Silverstein says most illegal immigrants find menial jobs in restaurant kitchens, parking garages, on farms, or in garment

Two Asian women ply their trade in a Chinatown garment factory. Some sources estimate that 50,000 illegal immigrants toil in 3,000 sweatshops in New York City alone.

factories. Because many employers know illegal workers are unlikely to complain to authorities, they often fail to provide safe and decent working conditions to illegal immigrants. He cites the exploitation of illegal female Chinese employees who manufacture blue jeans in New York as an example. According to Silverstein, these women may work up to 60 hours per week for less than $200, and they receive no health insurance or other benefits.[12]

Silverstein further notes that immigrants arrive in the United States from all over the world, but the great majority—about 80 percent—come from poor countries in Latin America and Asia. More than half of all illegal immigrants, he says, come from Mexico, where 40 percent of the population is unemployed and poverty is widespread. For these immigrants, Silverstein contends, "the economic allure of the United States is so strong that they may risk life and limb to get here."[13]

There is a great deal of disagreement as to whether these immigrants take jobs from American citizens. Immigration advocates argue that recent immigrants to the United States provide much of the cheap labor in this country, especially in farming states.[14] Writer José Armas, for example, cites a study that concludes, "Immigrants do not rob citizens of jobs but either expand employment niches or take jobs few Americans want."[15]

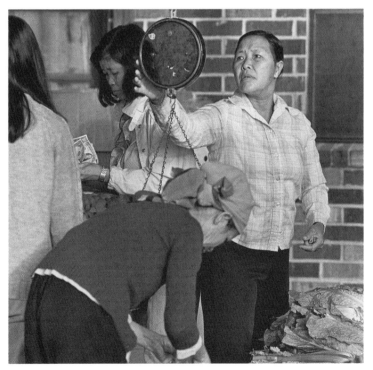

Vietnamese women buy and sell produce in a traditional outdoor market in New Orleans.

Patricia Harty, a critic of California's Proposition 187, writes, "While I know it is an oversimplification to say that America in denying its immigrants is denying its heritage, is it also oversimplifying the matter to ask whether Americans are willing to do jobs that the immigrants, illegal and otherwise, do? Are the rest of us waiting in line to pick grapes and tomatoes, to waitress, be nannies, busboys, doormen, and cab drivers? I don't think so."[16]

IMMIGRANTS AND WELFARE

Freddy Rios had heart surgery at Jackson Memorial Hospital in Miami in 1993. A year later, he was back in the emergency room, complaining of chest pain and fatigue. One nurse took his blood pressure, another fiddled with oxygen tubes and checked a heart monitor, and a doctor recorded Freddy's medical history while a Spanish-speaking resident interpreted. The taxpayers of Dade County, Florida, got the bill, because Freddy, from Nicaragua, was an illegal immigrant.[17] Freddy had sneaked into the U.S. five years earlier. In the meantime, he had fathered two children by an undocumented Nicaraguan woman. Because both children are U.S. citizens, they're entitled to the same social benefits as all other citizens.

Freddy's story, and others like it, have helped fuel the immigration debate. Many people believe that immigrants—especially illegal immigrants—are bloating the welfare system and draining U.S. resources. California governor Pete Wilson claims that social services for illegal immigrants cost his state $3 billion a year.[18] California state assemblyman Richard Mountjoy

Vietnamese refugee Duc Nguyen stacks noodles in the grocery store he owns. He also owns a restaurant, tailoring shop, film processing store, and video rental outlet in Seattle. His success is typical of refugees who have done well in the United States.

commented in 1993, "We've had a multibillion-dollar deficit three years in a row, and yet we continue to pay . . . for these illegal immigrants. We take better care of them than of our own people."[19]

José Armas calls that notion a myth. In fact, he says, only 4 percent of immigrants receive welfare aid. He cites a *Business Week* study that reported immigrants annually pay $90 billion in taxes but receive only $5 billion in welfare benefits.[20] An extensive *U.S. News & World Report* study of 1990 Census Bureau data seems to add weight to Armas's argument. *U.S. News* reports, "One of the most persistent myths about immigrants in America is that they are parasites who live on welfare provided by hard-working U.S. taxpayers."[21] Most immigrants don't get welfare, because they can't. Legal immigrants do not qualify for welfare programs for five years under the 1996 Welfare Reform Act, and illegal immigrants are denied all major social services except emergency medical care. In 1993, legal immigrants— nearly 9 percent of the country's population— accounted for only 5 percent of all families receiving federal welfare checks or food stamps. Those figures show that immigrants are less likely than other citizens to receive aid.[22] In 1996, food stamps were being used by 27 million American citizens (1 out of every 10 people), according to the Agriculture Department, which oversees the program.[23]

According to *U.S. News & World Report,* political refugees and elderly immigrants are exceptions to that

With his jacket hung on the wall of the building behind him, a sheet of plywood to block the wind (on his left), his tools and supplies on the sidewalk, Yok Ten Tam sews a new sole on a shoe. Although he speaks little English, he manages quite well at his outdoor "shop" in New York City.

rule. Refugees, typically from Communist countries, have quick access to welfare programs in the United States and usually make use of those programs. *U.S. News* listed the percentage of immigrants receiving welfare in relation to their place of birth. Cambodians topped the list at 28 percent. Immigrants from Laos and the ancient Hmong hill tribes of Southeast Asia came in a close second at 27 percent. Vietnamese placed near the middle of the list at 16 percent, Cubans at 10 percent, and Mexicans at 2 percent.[24]

Immigrants over 65 years of age receive welfare money under the federal Supplemental Security Income program. According to the *U.S. News* study, 65 percent of Laotians, 52 percent of Vietnamese, and 48 percent of former Soviets received such benefits in 1989 [the most recent figures available, based on 1990 census information].[25] Professor Norman Matloff of the University of California at Davis found that 55 percent of elderly Chinese immigrants in California were on welfare, while only 9 percent of California's older native-born residents received welfare.[26] Do numbers like these foster a general belief that SSI dollars are there for the taking and that immigrants will rush to grab them?

Ronald W. Wong, writing in *Asian Week*, bypasses the political and numerical arguments and cuts straight to the heart of what he perceives as the real issue. He writes:

> Even if each and every one of the current anti-immigrant proposals were adopted, immigrants would continue to flock to the United States. It is an economic reality that money, goods, services, and people will flock to wealthier countries. We see this migration even within the United States

Jewish refugees from the former Soviet Union shop at a local market in the Brighton Beach community of Brooklyn.

as thousands have fled California for jobs in other states. Unless Mexico and other lesser developed economies grow to equal that of the United States in terms of economic opportunity, there will always be large numbers who seek a better life in America.[27]

Wong makes a valid point. Are immigrants of the late twentieth and early twenty-first century really much different from the Irish, for example, who fled famine and poverty in the mid-1800s? Wong says, "Our elected officials must be held accountable for strengthening our economy, not for outdoing each other on unworkable and unconstitutional anti-immigrant

This young immigrant is one of the most popular merchants on the Lower East Side of New York. He sells paper cups full of shaved ice. On top of the ice, he pours sweet syrup of various flavors.

proposals. Let's work toward stopping the immigrant bashing and improving our economy, so everyone can enjoy the fruits of their labor."[28]

As long as the United States remains a vital economic power and as long as immigrants continue to arrive, there will probably be arguments about jobs, welfare programs, and the proper expenditure of taxpayers' money. Another matter of social significance is that of crime.

IMMIGRANTS AND CRIME

Have recent immigrants to the United States, especially illegal aliens, contributed to a rising crime rate, or are they being unfairly blamed for this issue? In 1995, Governor Pete Wilson wrote a letter to Attorney General

Janet Reno demanding that the federal government pay the cost of California's illegal immigrant criminals or "take custody of each and every one of them." He enclosed a list of 16,030 prisoners he says have been identified as illegal immigrants. According to Wilson and his supporters, illegal immigrants account for 20 percent of California's prison population.[29]

Ron K. Unz, owner of a computer software company, pointed out that "a recent *National Review* editorial made much of the statistic that 20 percent of California's prison inmates are immigrants. But this is hardly

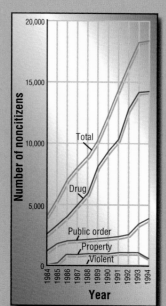

Noncitizens in Federal Prisons
1984-1994

•Between 1984 and 1994, the number of noncitizens serving a sentence of imprisonment in a federal prison increased an average of 15% annually— from 4,088 to 18,929; the overall federal prison population, by contrast, increased an average of 10% annually—from 31,105 to 87,437.

•55% of the noncitizens prosecuted in federal court during 1994 were in the United States illegally.

•During 1984 about 35% of noncitizens prosecuted in federal court were charged with a drug offense. By 1994, the proportion charged with a drug offense had increased to 45%.

•Nearly all (93%) of prosecutions for immigration offenses involved noncitizens.

•1.4% of noncitizens prosecuted in federal court were charged with a violent crime compared with 8.5% of citizens.

•Noncitizens convicted of a federal drug offense were more likely than citizens to have played a minor role in the drug conspiracy. About 29% of noncitizens convicted of a drug offense received a downward sentencing adjustment for "mitigating role," compared with 14% of U.S. citizens.

Source: U.S. Department of Justice, Bureau of Justice Statistics

surprising in a state where 20 percent of the residents are immigrants."[30] Unz then cited some statistics of his own. San Jose, California, he noted, is the 11th largest city in the nation and has a white (Anglo) population of less than 50 percent. The balance of the population consists of Asian and Hispanic immigrants, many of them illegal. Yet, Unz says, "San Jose has a flourishing economy, the lowest murder and robbery rates of any major city in America (less than one-fifth the rate in Dallas, for example), and virtually no significant ethnic conflict." In El Paso, Texas, the Hispanic population is 70 percent. Even so, Unz says, El Paso also has one of the lowest rates of serious crime, with a robbery rate "just half that of Seattle, an overwhelmingly white city of similar size."[31]

Statistics are frequently used to bolster or deflate arguments surrounding many issues, but how accurate

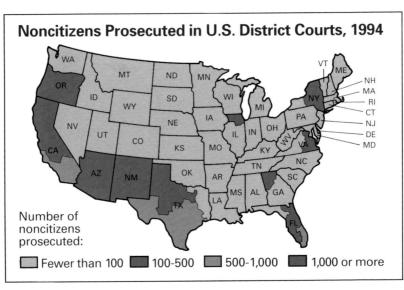

Noncitizens Prosecuted in U.S. District Courts, 1994

Number of noncitizens prosecuted:

☐ Fewer than 100 ■ 100–500 ▨ 500–1,000 ■ 1,000 or more

Source: U.S. Department of Justice, Bureau of Justice Statistics

and reliable are they? When dealing with the issues of immigrants and crime, statistics serve well as points of argument but offer little concrete evidence. *National Review* editors say, "Statistics on the national origin of state-prison inmates are fragmentary and unreliable in the extreme."[32] They note a *Wall Street Journal* article by John Miller of the Manhattan Institute for Policy Research (MIPR), which is based in New York. The Institute tries to create a better understanding of economic processes and the effects of government programs on American economics. Miller's article reported that 10.4 percent of California's inmates are illegal immigrants, while the California State Department of Corrections set the figure at more than 20 percent.[33]

National Review editors add, "We have no doubt that Mr. Miller agrees with us on this at least: that Americans ought to be able to find out whether or not immigrants contribute disproportionately to crime. But currently, the statistics are just not being kept."[34]

Author Peter Brimelow has taken a more speculative approach, asserting that immigrants and crime are somehow historically linked. Brimelow, author of *Alien Nation,* a book that is critical of U.S. immigration policy, cites crime as a "social consequence of immigration."[35] He begins with a quote from Ted Robert Gurr, Professor of Political Science at the University of Maryland and editor of *Violence in America: The History of Crime.* Gurr states that "the United States is in the grip of the third of three great crime waves. They began about 50 years apart—approximately 1850, 1900, and 1960—and each has lasted for 20 to 30 years."[36] According to Gurr, "America's three great crime waves can be linked to *immigration,* economic deprivation and war, which all interfere with the civilizing process . . . . *the first and second episodes of violent crime wound down as immigrants were incorporated into the expanding economy.*"[37] [Brimelow's italics]

Brimelow adds, "Obviously, the current crime wave cannot ebb if immigrants continue to arrive as fast as they are incorporated—or faster."[38] Here Brimelow cautions his readers, saying, "Note carefully: immigration is not the *only* cause of crime. It may not even be the major cause of crime. But it is a *factor.*"[39] As to hard evidence concerning immigrants and crime, Brimelow asserts that "news about immigrant crime is firmly in the unfit-to-print category. Researchers find that official figures on immigrant and ethnic crime patterns are rarely collected. Cities like New York, Chicago and San Francisco," Brimelow alleges, "have even instructed their employees not to cooperate with the INS. *There has been no serious academic study of the impact on crime of the Second Great Wave of Immigration.*"[40] [Brimelow's italics]

Tom Morganthau, who reviewed Brimelow's book for *Newsweek* magazine, accuses Brimelow, who was born in Britain but is now a U.S. citizen, of "racialism, if not racism."[41] Morganthau says Brimelow "thinks successful nationhood requires 'links by blood'" and "thinks race counts, though he never actually says other racial groups are inferior to whites. But he implies it, by rehashing tendentious [one-sided, biased] research on immigrant welfare dependency and the net economic burden on native-born citizens, and by making much of the irrelevant fact that immigrants now

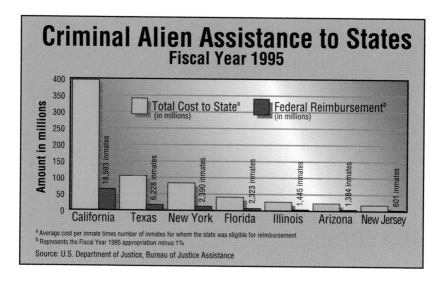

Criminal Alien Assistance to States
Fiscal Year 1995

- Total Cost to State[a] (in millions)
- Federal Reimbursement[b] (in millions)

California — 18,593 inmates
Texas — 6,228 inmates
New York — 2,390 inmates
Florida — 2,323 inmates
Illinois — 1,445 inmates
Arizona — 1,384 inmates
New Jersey — 601 inmates

[a] Average cost per inmate times number of inmates for whom the state was eligible for reimbursement
[b] Represents the Fiscal Year 1995 appropriation minus 1%

Source: U.S. Department of Justice, Bureau of Justice Assistance

compose 25 percent of the federal prison population."[42] Morganthau concludes, "Brimelow needs reminding that the melting pot still works—and that his alarmist views on race and ethnicity are exactly what his adoptive country is trying to outgrow."[43]

Vic Cox, author of *The Challenge of Immigration,* writes that ". . . blaming vulnerable, usually powerless groups for social and economic ills is a standard feature of the American political landscape. It goes back at least to the nativists of the last century, particularly when the charge is crime."[44] Cox concludes, "The racism is less blatant today, but vicious stereotypes are often based on isolated instances, and unrelated facts can be bent to create the appearance of truth."[45]

Crime is a legitimate social concern in America and a pressing issue among citizens and noncitizens alike. Whether immigrants—legal or illegal—have contributed to the problem remains unresolved.

As more and more immigrants from less familiar cultures arrive in the United States, many people fear the melting pot will turn into a pressure cooker.

ETHICAL, CULTURAL, AND MORAL CONSIDERATIONS

Many religious and civic leaders abhor anti-immigration movements. In a recent message to U.S. Episcopal dioceses, Edmund Browning, presiding bishop of the Episcopal Church, said, "I recognize that immigration is a complex issue which generates considerable public debate. As we deliberate on this issue, our fundamental responsibility as Christians remains. We must resist punishing victims who deserve our compassion. Denying basic services to individuals because of their immigration status does not advance the cause of sound public policy nor address the root causes of immigration: injustice, persecution, violence and a fundamental desire to be reunited with one's family."[1] Browning called Proposition 187 a "chilling message to newcomers that their presence is a threat and a burden."[2]

U.S. News & World Report explored the immigration issue in a comprehensive article titled "Shutting the

Golden Door." Author Robert Stevens states that elements of "economic fear, ethnic prejudice and politics as usual make the melting pot a pressure cooker."[3] Stevens notes that our country is "plunging into another divisive debate over immigration policy," but, he adds, our history is "littered" with such debates. Emotional self-examination and breast-beating over immigration usually erupt when three conditions are present: an unstable economy, a large influx of new and unfamiliar ethnic groups, and politicians who are willing and eager to exploit the issues.[4]

Congressman Lamar Smith is one of many politicians who have made immigration a key issue. "We have to gain control of our borders," he says. "There is nothing wrong with putting America first."[5] While

The increasing support for tighter immigration laws troubled Barbara Jordan, the late congresswoman from Texas and head of the United States Commission on Immigration Reform.

Mexican activists burn an effigy of Governor Pete Wilson along the Mexican border with California. They held the protest against Proposition 187 on October 29, 1994, just a few days before Californians approved it in the November election.

Smith's campaign remarks go directly to the practice of nativism, he is no doubt expressing the sentiments of his constituents, those who elected him to office.

Indeed, in late 1992, a *Los Angeles Times* poll reported that 82 percent of all Americans favor tighter immigration laws.[6] That poll and others like it troubled the late Texas representative Barbara Jordan, recent head of the U.S. Commission on Immigration Reform. Polls like these, she said, reflect "a heightened anti-immigration sentiment that is so discernible and identifiable that you can almost smell it."[7]

IMMIGRANTS AND AMERICA'S CULTURE

In addition to economic and political issues, there is also the issue of multiculturalism. Many people fear that new waves of immigrants, especially those since about 1980, have refused to assimilate—that is, to become like "us." They refuse to adopt American customs and attitudes. This refusal to assimilate could lead to separate and distinct cultures rather than one unified country.

Writer John O'Sullivan states bluntly that "immigration and the multiculturalism it feeds are threatening to dissolve the bonds of common nationhood and the underlying sense of a common national destiny, bringing forward the danger of a balkanized America."[8] To balkanize means to break up a group or region into small, often hostile units. "Only the politicians and intellectuals, including conservatives, are oblivious to the dangers, or persist in explaining them away," O'Sullivan adds. His statement attacks those who "argue that immigrants are a net economic and social benefit to America, that immigration is not a major contributor to America's cultural problems, and that immigrants and immigration are not at the core of America's identity as a nation."[9]

O'Sullivan argues that the arrival of more people from a variety of cultures "tends to sharpen the sense of ethnic difference among native Americans." This, he says, weakens the common national identity and the sense of civic solidarity. According to O'Sullivan, "In periods of little or no immigration, the common national identity asserts itself; in periods of high immigration, it retreats."[10]

To illustrate his point, O'Sullivan cites an *Atlantic Monthly* article by Roy Beck on the effects of immigration in the town of Wausau, Wisconsin.[11] According to the article, immigrant Hmong girls in Wausau schools have a high rate of underage pregnancy. However, school authorities have taken no action, nor do they plan to, because they feel early parenthood is part of Hmong culture.

"It scarcely matters," O'Sullivan says, "whether or not this judgment is correct; what the story illustrates is the nervousness of American culture faced with what it believes to be cultural diversity. Even on so painful a question as sex with minors, it hesitates to assert its own standards." And, says O'Sullivan, "those standards will consequently tend to fall into disuse."[12] In essence, O'Sullivan is saying that Americans are

Almost 10,000 people—mostly Hispanic—participated in what was called the largest naturalization event in American history. The event took place in the Orange Bowl in Miami, Florida.

abandoning traditional values in an effort to accommodate the cultural values, morals, and practices of foreigners who reside here.

David Cole disagrees and labels the current anti-
immigration mood "the new Know-Nothingism."[13] Cole
quotes one Know-Nothing who wrote in 1856, "Four-
fifths of the beggary and three-fifths of the crime spring
from our foreign population; more than half the public
charities, more than half the prisons and almshouses,
more than half the police and the cost of administering
criminal justice are for foreigners."[14] Cole believes "the
Know-Nothings have returned. As in the 1850s, the
movement is strongest where immigrants are most concentrated: California and Florida. The objects of prejudice are of course no longer Irish Catholics and
Germans; 140 years later, 'they' have become 'us.' The
new 'they'—because it seems 'we' must always have a
'they'—are Latin Americans (most recently, Cubans),
Haitians, and Arab-Americans, among others."[15]

The claim that aliens refuse to assimilate and deprive "us" of our cultural and political unity has been
made about every new group of immigrants to arrive
on U.S. shores. Cole says, "In most instances, such
claims are simply not true."[16] American culture, he
says, has been created, defined, and revised by people
who descended from immigrants. "Our society exerts
tremendous pressure to conform," Cole argues, and
cultural separatism rarely survives a generation. "But
more important," Cole continues, "even if this claim
were true, is this a legitimate rationale for limiting immigration in a society built on the values of pluralism
and tolerance?"[17]

WHAT ABOUT MORAL RESPONSIBILITY?

Does the United States have a moral responsibility to admit a certain number of legal immigrants and to provide basic services to undocumented immigrants? As a group, bishops of the Roman Catholic Church have criticized public officials who advocate closing U.S. borders. A policy statement adopted during a four-day meeting of the National Conference of Catholic Bishops declared, "The most vulnerable in the world—those with nowhere to lay their heads because of persecution and injustice—should not be denied justice, a safe haven, or a new life."[18] The bishops called an anti-immigration stance "unacceptable" in light of the church's social teachings. "As pastors, we are deeply

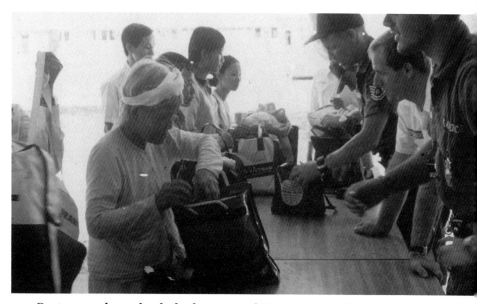

Custom workers check the baggage of Vietnamese refugees at a reception center on Wake Island, which is located in the Pacific Ocean, west of Hawaii.

More than 20 Romanian stowaways were found in containers aboard the American cargo ship Innovation *in April 1996. They were discovered en route between France and Boston, Massachusetts. U.S. immigration authorities led them ashore in handcuffs in Boston.*

concerned about the growing hostility toward immigrants evident now in some parts of our society and even, sad to say, supported by some public officials." Some public officials, the bishops noted, "are calling for public policies that tend to foster an attitude of selfishness and greed, racism and cultural bias. We must raise our collective voice, to protest this mentality and call for a change of heart and a renewed commitment as a nation in solidarity with immigrants and refugees."[19]

In his book *Alien Nation,* author Peter Brimelow also addresses the issue of morality by posing the following question:

> **If immigration is such a moral imperative, why
> don't the Mexicans/Chinese/Indians/Koreans/
> Japanese** (fill in any of the other recent top-ten
> suppliers of immigrants to the United States) **al-
> low it?** [Brimelow's bold type] Don't say: "These
> countries already have enough people." The
> United States already has more than all of them
> except mainland China and India. And don't say:
> "They're too poor." As we have seen, the whole
> economic theory of immigration, as developed by
> immigration enthusiasts, is that immigration does
> not displace workers: it complements them.[20]

Brimelow reports calling the embassy of the People's
Republic of China in Washington, D.C., to ask about
immigration. An official laughed and said, "China does
not accept any immigrants. We have a large enough
population."

Brimelow then cites the negative responses from
other embassies asked the same question. He also
states the number of immigrants each of those countries sent to the United States in 1992.

China	38,907
Mexico	91,332
South Korea	19,359
Philippines	61,022
Taiwan	16,344
Jamaica	18,915
Egypt	3,576
India	36,755[21]

Brimelow says, *"The world is laughing at America"*
[Brimelow's italics]. He suggests that "the critics of immigration adopt a name that has a long and honorable

New York City police raid a building that housed illegal Chinese immigrants in unsafe, overcrowded conditions.

role in American history. They should call themselves—'Patriots.'"[22]

While it may be true that Brimelow and other foes of immigration see themselves as patriots, it is equally true that advocates of immigration see themselves in the same light. Lenore Yarger, a member of the Dorothy Day Catholic Workers in Rock Island, Illinois, writes, "As Christians, we must decide how to respond. Leviticus speaks to us: 'When an alien resides with you in your land, you shall not oppress the alien. The alien who resides with you shall be to you as the citizen among you; you shall love the alien as yourself.'"[23]

Yarger then quotes Joan Maruskin, a Methodist seminarian. In 1993 Maruskin founded the group Golden Vision in support of the Chinese immigrants aboard the ill-fated *Golden Venture* that sank in New York Harbor. Maruskin charges that the American media painted an unrealistically gloomy picture of immigration. "The good news," Maruskin is quoted as saying, "is that immigrants are still welcome in the United States. The bad news is, no one is willing to say so."[24]

Cuban refugees, including a small girl, wave from a raft floating about 45 miles from Key West, Florida. All of the Cuban boat people picked up at sea are detained at the U.S. naval base at Guantanamo Bay, Cuba.

PUBLIC OPINION

"And what do Americans want?" author Peter Brimelow asks in regard to immigration. Then he answers his own question: "I don't believe, after long and careful inspection, that they want anything very terrible for their fellow human beings. They seem to me as if they would accept any immigrant, of any complexion including plaid, given minimum goodwill and good intentions. (Which, however, I also suspect are now often lacking.) But there are limits. Enough, as Americans invariably say in private conversation, is enough."[1]

Nathan Glazer, coeditor of *The Public Interest* (a Washington D.C.–based publication focusing on social, political, and economic policy), also comments on what he believes Americans want with regard to immigration policy. Glazer writes:

> My sense is that the state of American public opinion is now modestly restrictionist. The scale of immigration is larger than most people would choose, for a host of reasons: they don't think

America should become a country of mass immigration again, and see no good reason, economic or other, for this. They ask why the stream of immigration should be so unrepresentative [different in terms of race and culture] of the nation that already exists. They support the need to admit refugees. They are against illegal immigration, even though they may benefit from the services of such immigrants. They think immigration policies should reflect our compassion, our respect for human rights, the desire of immigrant neighbors to bring in parents, children and spouses, perhaps some brothers and sisters. They believe immigration polices should reflect our desire to improve the country—more of the kind of immigrants who become high-school class valedictorians and win science prizes.[2]

Glazer concludes, "That's about where I come out, too. There is no blueprint here, only a list of preferences that are not disreputable and should be respected. Whatever our policies are, I think our biggest problem will be to carry them out in a world in which so many see entry into the United States as a way of improving themselves."[3]

Here, Glazer has pointed his pen directly at the heart of the immigration problem and the core of the debate. In short, how does the United States establish a policy that would allow entry to a reasonable number of legal immigrants and refugees, while at the same time curtail the flood of illegal immigrants pouring into the United States from impoverished countries in Latin America, the Caribbean, and Asia?

Noted political commentator William F. Buckley Jr. says, "It is the consensus among thoughtful students of

the current problem (they include writers such as Peter Brimelow of *Forbes/National Review,* and politicians such as Pete Wilson of California) that the
legal-immigration quota is too high, that illegal immigration is too high, that cultural accommodations are
overindulgent, and that judicial affirmations [court rul-
ings] are here and there licentious [lacking legal or
moral restraints]."[4] Buckley says he and other
"thoughtful students" support "entirely defensible proposals" that call for

- reducing the legal-immigration quota for a
  dozen years or more until the existing pool is
  assimilated;
- cracking down on illegal immigrants through
  more effective repatriation [deportation], a
  closer guard on frontiers, and unlicensing
  [denying] welfare benefits for illegals;
- a drive against bilingual, let alone trilingual,
  education.

"The melting pot brew," Buckley says, "is all but
poisoned if the candidate for assimilation is not required to adjust to a common language."[5] Buckley's
proposals would likely find much support across
America. In late 1993 a *Time* magazine poll of more
than 1,100 Americans revealed that 73 percent of those
polled favored strictly limited immigration, while only
24 percent were in favor of keeping the door open to
immigration. Asked if they felt most immigrants were
coming into the United States legally or illegally,
64 percent said illegally and 24 percent said legally.[6]

John O'Sullivan offers his own theory for the current
negative feeling toward immigrants. O'Sullivan cites

Noted writer and political commentator William F. Buckley Jr. wants to reduce legal immigration and crack down on illegal aliens.

the "great waves" of immigration in the past and notes, "Any wave of immigration . . . has pushed public opinion firmly in favor of restrictions. Restrictionist legislation was firmly (and popularly) in place from 1925 to 1965. And public opinion polls have shown a steady two-thirds of Americans favoring less immigration since the mid-sixties."[7]

A *New York Times* editorial put the immigration problem in a unique perspective, saying: "There is a limit to our powers of assimilation, and when it is exceeded the country suffers from something very like indigestion."[8] Interestingly enough, that editorial was written over a century ago, in May 1880. Times have changed, but the passions, convictions, issues, and arguments surrounding immigration debate remain essentially the same.

Father Richard John Neuhaus, editor in chief of *First Things* (a publication addressing religious and public issues), agrees that there is overwhelming public support to tighten control over admission of legal immigrants and to cut illegal immigration to "near zero." According to Neuhaus, most people want to avoid the spread of multiculturalism and prevent immigrants from becoming dependent on welfare.

"There may also be strong support," Neuhaus adds, "for basing admission more on job skills and less on

Augustine Garcia (center) *is greeted by happy relatives after he was released from an INS detention center in Miami, Florida. He traveled from Cuba to Florida on a small boat with 16 other illegal Cuban immigrants.*

whether a would-be immigrant is a relative of some-body already here." He says, "Many Americans might be open to following Canada, requiring that relatives post a bond [pay a cash deposit to authorities] for im-migrants whom they sponsor, to ensure that they stay off welfare."[9] Currently, Canada accepts about 200,000 immigrants a year, more than half of them Asians.[10] As in the United States, Chinese immigration was barred by Canada for a period of time. However, Canada has since passed legislation that accepts immigrants with-out regard to ancestry, race, religion, or sex.[11]

THE POLLS

In the United States, public opinion polls support claims that Americans are in a foul mood where immi-gration is concerned. One such poll, conducted by *Time* magazine, revealed that 85 percent of those ques-tioned favor tough federal laws to reduce the number of immigrants who enter the United States illegally. At the same time, 60 percent would like changes in fed-eral law that would reduce the number of legal immi-grants.[12] In the same poll, 49 percent favored an amendment to prevent children born here from becom-ing U.S. citizens unless the parents were citizens as well, but 47 percent opposed such an amendment.

Exactly half (50 percent) of those polled said all U.S. citizens should be required to carry a national identifi-cation card, and 61 percent said the government should have more restrictions for immigrants who claim persecution in their own countries. Almost a third of those polled (29 percent) would like a fence along the entire border between the United States and

Mexico.[13] While the Immigration and Welfare Reform Bills of 1996 produced relatively minor changes in immigration policy, public opinion and pressure on legislators will probably generate additional policy changes in the future.

The questions posed by *Time*'s poll raise some additional questions. For example, even though half of those polled said they favor a national identification card, how many of those Americans would actually be willing or happy to submit to what many feel is a police state tactic if Congress were to pass such a law? How many would be willing to bear the financial burden of building and patrolling a fence between the United States and Mexico, if that fence were to become a reality? And would a fence actually stop illegal immigrants from Latin America who were determined to enter the United States?

The question concerning the Fourteenth Amendment raises several additional questions. Would children of legal immigrants (those who are legal residents but not yet citizens) be denied citizenship? Since a legal immigrant must reside in the United States for five years before becoming eligible for citizenship, when would the children of legal immigrants become eligible? A child of five would hardly be mature enough to qualify for a citizenship exam. And, as has been asked many times in the past, what exactly constitutes political persecution in another country?

The United States Coast Guard checks the credentials of new Cuban refugees.

WHAT IS YOUR OPINION?

Opinions regarding immigration may stem from economic, social, cultural, religious, moral, or even personal and emotional feelings. When you take the following opinion poll, consider your answers carefully. Perhaps you can debate the issues with other students. In the United States, more than in any other country, policymakers tend to base decisions on public opinion. Students, as the next generation of voters and taxpayers, will play a vital role in shaping the lives of future immigrants. Many students are children of Latino, Asian, African, or European immigrants. Your collective experiences, feelings, and opinions will eventually chart America's course on this compelling social issue.

WHERE DO YOU STAND?

Is the United States taking in more immigrants than it can handle? Should our doors be open to anyone who wants to make a living here? The following poll is reprinted with permission from *Scholastic Update*.[1] Answer the questions on a separate sheet of paper, then compare your opinions with those of other people around the country.

1. Do you think immigration has been a good thing or a bad thing for the United States in the past?
2. Do you think immigration is a good thing or a bad thing for this country today?
3. Do you think the United States is still as much a melting pot as it used to be, or do immigrants today maintain their own national identity more strongly?
4. Do you approve or disapprove of the way the president is handling the issue of illegal immigration?
5. Do you agree or disagree that immigrants take the jobs of U.S. workers?
6. Do you agree or disagree that immigrants work hard—often taking jobs that Americans don't want?
7. Do you agree or disagree that many immigrants wind up on welfare and raise taxes for Americans?
8. How concerned are you that immigrants may help terrorists?
   a) very concerned; b) somewhat concerned; c) not too concerned; or d) not at all concerned.
9. Should the United States continue to be more lenient toward people immigrating to escape political oppression than toward people immigrating for economic reasons?
10. How concerned are you that immigrants may create problems for schools?
    a) very concerned; b) somewhat concerned; c) not too concerned; or d) not at all concerned.
11. Some people feel that only English should be used in American schools and on public signs and official government documents. Others support the use of a second language in some areas to help immigrants participate in education, business, and public life. What is your view?

***This Asian family poses in front of the Statue of Liberty—
still a powerful symbol.***

12. Do you think it should be easier or more difficult for people from China to immigrate to the United States?

13. Do you think it should be easier or more difficult for people from Latin America to immigrate to the United States?

14. Do you think it should be easier or more difficult for people from Eastern Europe to immigrate to the United States?

15. Do you think it should be easier or more difficult for people from the Middle East to immigrate to the United States?

POLL ANSWERS

Here's how Americans responded to the questions posed above.[2] Results were taken from a nationwide poll conducted by *Newsweek* magazine and Princeton Survey Research Associates in July 1993 and reprinted by *Scholastic Update*. (Percentages don't always add up to 100 because some people expressed no opinion.)

1. 59 percent said immigration has been a good thing in the past; 31 percent said bad.
2. 29 percent said immigration is a good thing for the country today; 60 percent said bad.
3. 66 percent said recent immigrants maintain their national identity more strongly; 20 percent said the United States is still a melting pot.
4. 39 percent approved; 38 percent disapproved.
5. 62 percent agreed; 34 percent disagreed.
6. 78 percent agreed; 18 percent disagreed.
7. 59 percent agreed; 33 percent disagreed.
8. 44 percent said they were "very concerned" that immigrants may help terrorists; 30 percent were "somewhat concerned 16 percent were "not too concerned"; 8 percent were "not at all concerned."
9. 53 percent said the United States should continue to be more lenient; 36 percent disagreed.
10. 31 percent of Americans said they were "very concerned" that immigrants may create problems for schools; 31 percent said they were "somewhat concerned"; 24 percent said they were "not too concerned"; 10 percent said they were "not at all concerned."
11. 51 percent said they believed only English should be used in school and for official business; 47 percent said they supported the use of a second language in some areas.
12. 32 percent of those surveyed said easier; 49 percent said more difficult; 10 percent said it should remain about the same.

13. 30 percent said easier; 47 percent said more difficult; 14 percent said it should remain about the same.
14. 39 percent said easier; 39 percent said more difficult; 12 percent said it should remain about the same.
15. 18 percent said easier; 61 percent said more difficult; 11 percent said it should remain about the same.

QUESTIONS TO PONDER

Look at poll questions 1 and 2. The opinions of those surveyed are almost exactly reversed regarding immigration in the past and immigration now. What do you think has caused this shift?

Read questions 5, 6, and 7 again and review the answers. Do you find it curious that 62 percent of those

Cultural diversity exists in the United States. Is it a blessing or a burden?

surveyed believe immigrants take jobs from U.S. workers, while at the same time an overwhelming majority
(78 percent) think immigrants work hard and take jobs
Americans *don't* want? If immigrants do work hard at
jobs rejected by Americans, would you still agree with
the survey result to question 7? According to their responses, well over half of those surveyed feel many immigrants end up on welfare. What do you think?

The survey results for questions 12 through 15 provide an interesting look at how Americans perceive
others. What do you think the answers say about attitudes toward different peoples, especially those from
China, Latin America, and the Middle East? Why are
Americans generally more accepting of people from
Eastern Europe? What do you think are some reasons
for the attitudes expressed in the poll?

THE NEXT CHAPTER

Our country's brief history, begun and fueled by immigrants, has traveled an illustrious but rocky road. Our
population has swelled to nearly 260 million people.
Some say, "This is all we can accommodate—shut the
door." Others point to America's golden door and say,
"This is our heritage—this is what built America.
Come, join us."

The United States has taken in more immigrants
than any other country on earth. Perhaps we should
ask ourselves why. Do people in other lands see opportunities for economic advancement and personal and
political expression that their own countries don't offer? If that's true, should we use more resources for the
economic, political, and social development of other

countries, thereby curbing the flow of immigrants to the United States? Do we, as descendants of immigrants, have a moral or civic duty to open our door to immigrants? What will be the consequences if we open the door or if we slam it shut? The final answers to this chapter will likely be written by you and your generation. And then, probably a new chapter will begin.

As Bernard Weisberger wrote in *American Heritage,* "So it is that immigration regularly returns to the news. It always has. It always does."[3]

Resources to Contact

American Immigration Control
  Foundation (AICF)
Box 525, Main Street
Montery, VA 24465
PH: 703 468-2022

Americans for Immigration Control
  (AIC)
725 Second Street NE
Suite 370A
Washington, DC 20002
PH: 202 543-3719
FX: 202 543-5911

Center for Immigrants' Rights (CIR)
48 St. Mark's Place, 4th Floor
New York, NY 10003
PH: 212 505-6890
FX: 212 995-5876

Emerald Isle Immigration Center
  (EIIC)
5926 Woodside Avenue
Woodside, NY 11377
PH: 718 478-5502
FX: 718 446-3727

Emergency Committee to Suspend
  Immigration (ECSI)
P. O. Box 1211
Marietta, GA 30061
PH: 770 422-1180

Federation for American Immigration
  Reform (FAIR)
1666 Connecticut Avenue NW
Suite 400
Washington, DC 20009
PH: 1-800 395-0890
FX: 202 387-3447

National Immigration Forum (NIF)
220 Eye Street NE
Suite 220
Washington, DC 20002
PH: 202 544-0004
FX: 202 544-1905

National Immigration Law Center
  (NILC)
1636 West Eighth Street
Suite 205
Los Angeles, CA 90017
PH: 213 487-2531
FX: 213 384-4899

National Network for Immigrant and
  Refugee Rights (NNIRR)
310 Eighth Street, No. 307
Oakland, CA 94607
PH: 510 465-1984
FX: 510 465-7548

U.S. English, Inc.
818 Connecticut Avenue NW
Suite 200
Washington, DC 20006
PH: 202 833-0100
FX: 202 833-0108

Endnotes

CHAPTER 1: THE IMMIGRATION DILEMMA

[1] Quoted by Bernard A. Weisberger, "A Nation of Immigrants," *American Heritage*, February/March 1994, 80.

[2] "America's Immigration Challenge," *Time* Special Issue, Fall 1993, 9.

[3] From Emma Lazarus, "The New Colossus," inscribed on the base of the Statue of Liberty, 1903.

CHAPTER 2: WHO ARE THEY AND WHERE DO THEY COME FROM?

[1] Brent Ashabranner, *Still a Nation of Immigrants* (New York: Cobblehill Books, 1993), 15.

[2] Gerald Leinwand, *American Immigration* (New York: Franklin Watts, 1995), 15.

[3] John Elson, "The Great Migration," *Time* Special Issue, Fall 1993, 28.

[4] Leinwand, 15.

[5] Ibid., 23.

[6] Elson, 30.

[7] Leinwand, 24.

[8] Weisberger, 80.

[9] Leinwand, 26.

[10] Ibid.

[11] Ibid.

[12] Ashabranner, 15.

[13] Leinwand, 33.

[14] Ibid.

[15] Ibid.

[16] Elson, 31–32.

[17] Ibid., 32.

[18] Ashabranner, 18.

[19] Weisberger, 81.

[20] Leinwand, 35.

[21] Weisberger, 81.

[22] Elson, 32.

[23] *Columbia-Viking Desk Encyclopedia,* 3d ed., 794.

[24] Elson, 33.

[25] Vic Cox, *The Challenge of Immigration* (Springfield, New Jersey: Enslow, 1995), 27.

[26] Ibid.

[27] Ashabranner, 14.

[28] Leinwand, 37.

[29] Ibid., 45.

[30] Ibid., 52.

[31]Weisberger, 86.

[32]Leinwand, 64.

[33]Ashabranner, 21.

[34]Weisberger, 86.

[35]Leinwand, 69.

[36]Ibid.

[37]Ashabranner, 22.

[38]Leinwand, 72.

[39]Ibid., 72–73.

[40]Ibid., 73.

[41]Weisberger, 87.

[42]Ibid., 88.

[43]Ibid., 89.

[44]Ibid., 88.

[45]Ibid., 89.

CHAPTER 3: IMMIGRATION POLICY

[1]Pauline Arrillaga, "Welfare Changes Will Hit Hard in Poor County," Peoria *Journal Star,* 30 September 1996.

[2]Carlos Angulo, legislative aide to Senator Paul Simon of Illinois, telephone interview, 9 October 1996.

[3]Carol Jouzaitis, "Cuts in U.S. Food Aid Likely to Tighten Belt for Millions," *Chicago Tribune,* 18 August 1996.

[4]Ibid.

[5]Arrillaga.

[6]Mary Jacoby, "Immigration Bill Targets Legals, Too," *Chicago Tribune,* 25 September 1996.

[7]Ibid.

[8]Ibid.

[9]Ibid.

[10]David Jackson, "Give Us Your Tired, Your Poor, Your Votes," *Chicago Tribune,* 27 August 1996.

[11]Ibid.

[12]Melita Marie Garza, "User-Friendly Path to Citzenship," *Chicago Tribune,* 8 April 1996.

[13]Ibid.

[14]Myles Gordon, "The Golden Door," *Scholastic Update,* 19 November 1994, 5.

[15]Judy Mark, National Immigration Forum, Washington, D.C., telephone interview, 9 October 1996.

[16]Karl Kaufmann, Legislative Director for U.S. Representative Bill McCollum, telephone interview, 9 October 1996.

[17]Fedelius Kuo, "Welfare Reform: Politically Correct Immigration Bashing," *Northwest Asian Weekly,* 2 July 1994.

[18]Ibid.

CHAPTER 4: CRISIS IN CALIFORNIA

[1]"The Failure and Success of Prop. 187," *Chicago Tribune,* 1 December 1995.

[2]Ibid.

[3]Ibid.

[4]William McGowan, "Crisis in California," *Scholastic Update,* 19 November 1993, 12.

[5]Ibid.

[6]Ibid.

[7]Ibid.

[8]Ibid.

[9]*Information Please Almanac* (Boston: Houghton Mifflin, 1996), 797.

[10]Ibid., 807.

[11]McGowan, 12.

[12]Karen Brandon, "Wilson Holds Fast to Immigration Issue," *Chicago Tribune,* 7 January 1996.

[13]Ibid.

[14]Bill Hughes, "Opinion: The Immigration Conundrum," *Oakland Post,* 20 July 1994.

[15]Ibid.

[16]Ibid.

[17]Ibid.

[18]Gary S. Becker, "Prop. 187 Is Fine—Now Rewrite Federal Law, Too," *Business Week,* 9 January 1995, 26.

[19]Ibid.

[20]David Miller, "Jews Join United Front against Anti-Immigration Bias," *Northern California Jewish Bulletin,* 8 October 1993, 3.

[21]Ibid.

[22]Brandon, 10.

CHAPTER 5: BOAT AND BORDER PEOPLE

[1]Cox, 18.

[2]Ibid.

[3]Ibid.

[4]Ibid., 20.

[5]Ibid.

[6]Karen N. Peart, "Borderline Calls," *Scholastic Update,* 19 November 1993, 23.

[7]Leinwand, 100.

[8]Ashabranner, 45.

[9]Peart, 3.

[10]John O'Sullivan, "America's Identity Crisis," *National Review,* 21 November 1994, 44.

[11]Ibid.

[12]David Cole, "Five Myths about Immigration," *The Nation,* 17 October 1994, 410.

133

[13]Ibid., 412.

[14]Ibid.

[15]Arrillaga, 2.

[16]Peart, 22.

[17]Ibid.

[18]O'Sullivan, 40.

[19]Ibid.

[20]Herbert Buchbaum, "An Immigrant's Story," *Scholastic Update,* 19 November 1993, 10.

CHAPTER 6: IMMIGRANTS AND THE U.S. ECONOMY: JOBS, WELFARE, CRIME

[1]Ken Silverstein, "The Labor Debate," *Scholastic Update,* 19 November 1993, 17.

[2]Cole, 410.

[3]Ibid.

[4]Ibid.

[5]Leinwand, 116.

[6]Ibid.

[7]Paul Recer for the Associated Press, "Report Sees Foreign Doctors as Threat," Peoria *Journal Star,* 24 January 1996.

[8]Ibid.

[9]Ibid.

[10]Ibid.

[11]Silverstein, 17.

[12]Ibid.

[13]Ibid.

[14]"Immigration Watchdog Cites Statistics and Spreads Hysteria," *News India,* 15 April 1993, 54.

[15]José Armas, "Immigration Facts and Fantasies," *El Sol Del Valle,* 1 January 1994, 148, 1.

[16]Patricia Harty, "The First Word: No Immigrants Need Apply," *Irish American,* X, no. 5, 31 October 1994, 6.

[17]Steven V. Roberts, "Shutting the Golden Door," *U.S. News & World Report,* 3 October 1994, 36.

[18]Peart, 23.

[19]Silverstein, 17.

[20]Armas, 1.

[21]Dorian Friedman and Penny Loeb, "The Myth of the Parasites," *U.S. News & World Report,* 3 October 1994, 38.

[22]Ibid.

[23]Jouzaitis, 3.

[24]Friedman and Loeb, 38.

[25]Ibid.

[26]Ibid.

[27]Ronald W. Wong, "Eye on Politics: Fear and Loathing Fuel Anti-Immigration Sentiment," *Asian Week,* 22 October 1993, 11.

[28]Ibid.

[29]Brandon, 10.

[30]Ron K. Unz, "Value Added," *National Review,* 7 November 1994, 58.

[31]Ibid.

[32]"Immigration Battle Lines," *National Review,* 11 July, 1994, 12.

[33]Ibid., 14.

[34]Ibid.

[35]Peter Brimelow, *Alien Nation* (New York: Random House, 1995), 182.

[36]Ibid.

[37]Ibid.

[38]Ibid.

[39]Ibid.

[40]Ibid.

[41]Tom Marganthau, "Fear of an Immigrant Nation," *Newsweek,* 8 May 1995, 63.

[42]Ibid.

[43]Ibid.

[44]Cox, 95.

[45]Ibid.

CHAPTER 7: ETHICAL, CULTURAL, AND MORAL CONSIDERATIONS

[1]Edmund Browning, "California Proposition Is Alien to the Gospel Mandate," *Anglican Advance,* February 1995, 3.

[2]Ibid.

[3]Roberts, 36.

[4]Ibid.

[5]Ibid.

[6]Ibid.

[7]Ibid.

[8]O'Sullivan, 76.

[9]Ibid., 36.

[10]Ibid., 40.

[11]Ibid.

[12]Ibid.

[13]Cole, 410.

[14]Ibid.

[15]Ibid.

[16]Ibid., 412.

[17]Ibid.

[18]"Bishops Warn against Anti-Immigrant Views," *Christian Century,* 8 December 1993, 1232.

[19]Ibid., 1233.

[20]Brimelow, 250–251.

[21]Ibid., 252–53.

[22]Ibid., 254.

[23]Lenore Yarger, "Yearning to Be Free: Why the Cry of Chinese Immigrants Is So Compelling," *The Other Side,* March/April 1995, 18.

[24]Ibid.

CHAPTER 8: PUBLIC OPINION

[1]Brimelow, xviii.

[2]Nathan Glazer, "The Closing Door: Restricting Immigration," *Current,* July/August 1994, 14.

[3]Ibid.

[4]William F. Buckley Jr., "On the Right: Yes, Immigration Reform." *National Review,* 15 August 1994, 79.

[5]Ibid.

[6]David Aikman and David S. Jackson, "Not Quite So Welcome Anymore," *Time,* Special Issue, Fall 1993, 11.

[7]John O'Sullivan, "John O'Sullivan Replies," *National Review,* 6 February 1995, 80.

[8]Aikman and Jackson, 10.

[9]Richard John Neuhaus, "Alien Nation," *National Review,* 6 February 1995, 62.

[10]*World Book Encyclopedia,* 1996 ed., s.v. "immigration."

[11]Ibid.

[12]Aikman and Jackson, 11.

[13]Ibid., 12.

CHAPTER 9: WHAT IS YOUR OPINION?

[1]*Newsweek* magazine and Princeton Survey Research Associates, "Where Do You Stand?" *Scholastic Update,* 19 November 1993, 4.

[2]*Newsweek* magazine and Princeton Survey Research Associates, "Poll Answers," *Scholastic Update,* 19 November 1993, 24.

[3]Weisberger, 76.

Glossary

alien: a resident born in or belonging to another country who has not acquired citizenship by naturalization; a foreigner

asylum: a refuge granted an alien by a sovereign state on its own territory

constituencies: a body of constituents; the voters or residents in a district represented by an elective officer

deportation: the lawful expulsion of a person from a state

emigrants: people who leave one country to establish residence in another. The prefix e- means out of and the prefix im- means into. Therefore the same person is both an emigrant from the country being left and an immigrant in the country being entered.

illegal immigrants: people who enter a new country without the knowledge or permission of that country's government

immigrants: people who enter a new country intending to establish permanent residence there

initiative: a procedure by which a specified number of voters may propose a statute, constitutional amendment, or ordinance, and compel a popular vote on its adoption

multiculturalism: the preservation of different cultures or cultural identities within a unified society, as a state or nation

refugees: people who leave their home countries because of war, famine, or persecution and seek admission to a new country

resident: a physician who joins the medical staff of a hospital as a salaried employee for a specified period to gain advanced training, usually in a particular field, being a full-time attendant at the hospital and often living on the premises; one who resides in a place

subcultures: groups having social, economic, ethnic, or other traits distinctive enough to distinguish them from others within the same culture or society

visa: an official document which allows people to visit a country other than their own for a specified period of time

Bibliography

Aikman, David, and David Jackson. "Not Quite So Welcome Anymore." *Time* 142, Special Issue (Fall 1993): 10–12.

"America's Immigration Challenge," *Time* 142, Special Issue (Fall 1993): 3–9.

Armas, José. "Immigration Facts and Fantasies." *El Sol Del Valle* 148 (12 January 1994): 1.

Auerbach, Stuart. "OD'd on MDs." *The Washington Post,* National Weekly Edition (29 January–4 February 1996): 34.

Becker, Gary S. "Prop. 187 Is Fine—Now Rewrite Federal Law, Too." *Business Week* (9 January 1995): 26.

"Bishops Warn against Anti-Immigration Views." *Christian Century* (8 December 1993): 1232–33.

Brandon, Karen. "Wilson Holds Fast to Immigration Issue." *Chicago Tribune* (7 January 1996): sec. 1, 10.

Brimelow, Peter. *Alien Nation.* New York: Random House, 1995.

Browning Edmund. "California Proposition Is Alien to the Gospel Mandate." *Anglican Advance* (February 1995): 3.

Buchbaum, Herbert. "An Immigrant's Story." *Scholastic Update* 126, no. 6 (19 November 1993): 8–11.

Buckley, William F. Jr. "On the Right: Yes, Immigration Reform." *National Review* (15 August 1994): 78–79.

Burne, R. E. "Don't Slam America's Golden Door." *U.S. Catholic* 58 (November 1993): 2.

Christopher, W. "FY 1994 Refugee Admissions." *U.S. Department of State Dispatch* 4, no. 40 (4 October 1993): 673–674.

"Clinton Goes after Illegal Immigrants." *Chicago Tribune* (7 May 1994): sec. 1, 6.

Cole, David. "Five Myths about Immigration." *The Nation* (17 October 1994): 410.

"Doublespeak from Clinton?" *Miami Times* 70, no. 12 (19 November 1992).

Duttma, Ruma. "The Worst Kind of Exploitation." *News India* 22, no. 21 (22 May 1992): 54.

Elson, John. "The Great Migration." *Time* 142, Special Issue (Fall 1993): 28–33.

Europa, Prudencio R. "Point Blank: Americans Are All Immigrants." *Filipino Reporter* 21, no. 15 (14 April 1994): 19.

"The Failure and Success of Prop 187." *Chicago Tribune* (1 December 1995).

Friedman, Dorian, and Penny Loeb. "The Myth of the Parasites." *U.S. News & World Report* (3 October 1994): 38.

Glazer, Nathan. "The Closing Door: Restricting Immigration." *Current* (July/August 1994): 11–15.

Gordon, Myles. "The Golden Door." *Scholastic Update* 126, no. 6 (19 November 1993): 3–5.

"The Great Immigration Debate." *Chicago Tribune* (24 June 1995).

"The Haiti Impasse." *Miami Times* 71, no. 44 (14 July 1994).

Harty, Patricia. "The First Word: No Immigrants Need Apply." *Irish American* 10, no. 5 (31 October 1994): 6.

Hughes, Bill. "Opinion: The Immigration Conundrum." *Oakland Post* 31, no. 15 (20 July 1994).

"Immigration Battle Lines." *National Review* (11 July 1994), 10–14.

"Immigration Debate." *America* (9 October 1993): 3.

"Immigration Watchdog Cites Statistics and Spreads Hysteria." *News India* 23, no. 16 (16 April 1993): 54.

"In Our Opinion: Policy Change Needed." *Call and Post* (Cleveland) 78, no. 2 (14 January 1993): 4A.

Katzberg, William. "Closer View: Can We Control Our Porous Borders?" *Jewish Journal* (21 July 1994): 30A.

Kuo, Fidelius. "Welfare Reform: Politically Correct Immigrant Bashing." *Northwest Asian Weekly* 13, no. 26 (2 July 1994): 1.

"The Labor Debate." *Scholastic Update* 126, no. 6 Teacher's Edition (19 November 1993): 3.

Lee, Brian. "Immigration: An Illinois Portrait." *Illinois Issues* 22, no. 1 (January 1996): 17–21.

McGowan, William. "Crisis in California." *Scholastic Update* 126, no. 6 (19 November 1993): 12–13.

Miller, David. "Jews Join United Front against Anti-Immigration Bias." *Northern California Jewish Bulletin* 142, no. 38 (8 October 1993): 3.

Morganthau, Tom. "America: Still a Melting Pot." *Newsweek* (9 August 1993): 16–23.

_____. "Fear of an Immigrant Nation." *Newsweek* (8 May 1995): 61–63.

Myers, Ched. "Outsiders Cannot Defile." *The Other Side* 31, no. 2 (March/April 1995): 13–15, 19.

Neuhaus, Richard John. "Alien Nation." *National Review* (6 February 1995): 62–66.

Newsweek magazine and Princeton Survey Research Associates. "Poll Answers." *Scholastic Update* 126, no. 6 (19 November 1993): 24.

Newsweek magazine and Princeton Survey Research Associates. "Where Do You Stand?" *Scholastic Update* 126, no. 6 (19 November 1993): 4.

Olson, Todd. "Coming to America." *Scholastic Update* 126, no. 6 (19 November 1993): 18–21.

O'Sullivan, John. "America's Identity Crisis." *National Review* (21 November 1994): 36–45, 76.

_____. "John O'Sullivan Replies." *National Review* (6 February 1995): 66, 80.

Peart, Karen N. "Borderline Calls." *Scholastic Update* 126, no. 6 (19 November 1993): 22–23.

Pena, Albert. "Immigrant Bashing." *La Prensa de San Antonio* 45, no. 50 (17 June 1994): 2A.

Recer, Paul, for Associated Press. "Report Sees Foreign Doctors as Threat." Peoria *Journal Star* (24 January 1996): A2.

"Reform or Resentment?" *Commonweal* 122. no. 1 (13 January 1995): 3–4.

Roberts, Steven V., et al. "Shutting the Golden Door." *U.S. News & World Report* (3 October 1994): 36–40.

Silverstein, Ken. "The Labor Debate." *Scholastic Update* 126, no. 6 (19 November 1993): 16–17.

Ting, Jan C. "The Door Stays Closed for Chinese." *Asian Week* 16, no. 3 (9 September 1994): 2.

Unz, Ron K. "Value Added." *National Review* (7 November 1994): 56–58.

Weisberger, Bernard A. "A Nation of Immigrants." *American Heritage* 45 (February/March 1994): 75–91.

Wong, Ronald W. "Eye on Politics: Fear and Loathing Fuel Anti-Immigrant Sentiment." *Asian Week* 15, no. 9 (22 October 1993): 11.

Yang, Catherine. "Clinton Could Wind Up Looking Like the Heavy on Immigration." *Business Week* (30 January 1995): 45.

Yarger, Lenore. "Yearning to Be Free: Why the Cry of Chinese Immigrants Is So Compelling." *The Other Side* 31, no. 2 (March/April 1995): 16–18.

Index

About the Author

Robert Morrow is a news reporter for the Peoria *Journal Star.* He has authored many magazine articles, several children's stories, and a college-level text. His cats, Beauregard and Fuzz, were the inspiration for two short stories published in *Cricket* magazine.

Although he keeps returning to journalism, Morrow has been—at various times in his life—a farmer, a soldier, a cheese salesman, a luxury car salesman, a college teacher, and a ranch foreman. His hobbies, which are as varied as his careers, include building and flying radio-controlled model airplanes, antique car restoration, music, theater, and reading.

Photo Acknowledgments

AP/Wide World Photos, 54, 57 (top), 60, 62, 64, 70, 73, 74, 84; Archive Photos, 23; Archive Photos/American Stock, 33 (bottom); Archive Photos/SAGA/Frank Capri, 118; California State Library, 30; Calumet Regional Archives, Indiana University Northwest, 81; Corbis-Bettmann, 10, 14, 33 (top), 110; H.J. Heinz Company, 28; Independent Picture Service, 31; © Richard B. Levine, 44, 102, 112; Library of Congress, 8, 18, 20, 24, 36; Copyright, 1994. Paul Conrad. Dist. by Los Angeles Times Syndicate. Reprinted by permission, 6; National Archives, Photo No. 210–G–2–C423, 39; National Archives of Canada/Neg. No. PA118768, 19; Reuters/Bettmann, 69, 78, 105; Reuters/Blake Sell/Archive Photos, 114; Reuters/John Gibbons/Archive Photos, 66, 67; © Frances M. Roberts, 11, 65, 82 (both); Royal Museum of Central Africa, 16; Smithsonian Institution, 26; UPI/Bettmann, 37, 43, 76 (top), 89, 90, 95, 96, 104, 119; UPI/Corbis-Bettmann, 13, 46, 52–53, 76 (bottom), 92, 93, 107; U.S. Air Force, 109; U.S. Coast Guard, 122; Visuals Unlimited, 35 (both) [Historic VU], 40 and 86 [© Mark E. Gibson], 57 (bottom) [© John Sohlden], 79 [© M. Long], 87 [Science VU], 125 and 127 [© Jeff Greenberg].

Front cover photos: © Richard B. Levine, center; Reuters/Blake Sell/ Archive Photos, bottom left; UPI/Corbis-Bettmann, bottom right and top. Back cover photo: © Richard B. Levine